Directing
Professionally

INTRODUCTIONS TO THEATRE

Series Editor: Jim Volz, California State University, Fullerton, USA

This series of textbooks provides a practical introduction to core areas of theatre and performance and has been designed to support semester teaching plans. Each book offers case studies and international examples of practice and will equip undergraduate students and emerging theatre professionals with the understanding and skills necessary to succeed—whether in study or in the entertainment industry.

Introduction to the Art of Stage Management:
A Practical Guide to Working in the Theatre and Beyond
Michael Vitale
ISBN 978-1-4742-5720-6

Introduction to Arts Management
Jim Volz
ISBN 978-1-4742-3978-3

Directing Professionally

A Practical Guide to Developing a Successful Career in Today's Theatre

Kent Thompson

methuen | drama

LONDON • NEW YORK • OXFORD • NEW DELHI • SYDNEY

METHUEN DRAMA

Bloomsbury Publishing Plc

50 Bedford Square, London, WC1B 3DP, UK

1385 Broadway, New York, NY 10018, USA

BLOOMSBURY, METHUEN DRAMA and the Methuen Drama logo are
trademarks of Bloomsbury Publishing Plc

First published in Great Britain 2019

Cover design: www.ironicitalics.com

Cover photograph © Sam Adams

A catalogue record for this book is available from the British Library.

A catalog record for this book is available from the Library of Congress.

ISBN: HB: 978-1-4742-8877-4
       PB: 978-1-4742-8876-7
       ePDF: 978-1-4742-8875-0
       eBook: 978-1-4742-8878-1

Series: Introductions to Theatre

Typeset by RefineCatch Limited, Bungay, Suffolk
Printed and bound in Great Britain

To find out more about our authors and books visit www.bloomsbury.com
and sign up for our newsletters.

For Kathleen

Contents

Part I Entering the Theatre Field

1 The Big Leap 3

2 Understanding the Business of Theatre 19

Part II Your First Professional Job

3 Interviewing for the Job 27

Acknowledgments

To Jim Volz for making this project happen. His encouragement, professional guidance, editorial experience, faith, **and** patience were invaluable in the writing of this book. To Gavin Cameron-Webb for his careful reading and sharp editorial eye, as well as his keen advice and constant support throughout the process. To the many directors, playwrights, artistic directors, and theatre professionals who answered emails and phone calls, gave interviews, debated ideas, or made comments for the book. Finally, to the many artists who have made my life as a director inspiring and gratifying.

Introduction

Directing for the professional theatre takes artistry, passion, fortitude, ingenuity, boundless curiosity, a gift for persuasion, and effective leadership (not to mention good luck). If you're reading this book, you already know that the professional theatre is an intensely competitive field. To overcome its unpredictability and tough working conditions, you must be driven to direct, which requires unflagging optimism and an unreasonable love for the stage. Early in my professional directing career, I had a rare opportunity to talk with Michael Bogdanov (1938–2017), the Welsh director. During a casual conversation with a group of assistant directors at the Stratford Festival in Canada, Bogdanov suggested that every director needed a dose of madness to succeed. Not insanity, but a measure of irrational inspiration. Bogdanov was a hugely prolific, widely acclaimed (and sometimes widely denounced) international theatre and opera director. He directed for the Royal Shakespeare Company, the Royal National Theatre, the Royal Opera House, Vienna's Burg Theatre, La Scala, Sydney Opera House, The Guthrie Theatre as well as on Broadway and in the West End. He founded the English Shakespeare Company with Michael Pennington and won an Olivier Award for his seven-play history cycle, *The Wars of the Roses*. He eschewed the conventional or intellectual approaches to classics and strove to create performances "for the people who have never been to the theatre before." His shows were audacious, exuberant, eclectic, political, and big-hearted, earning him the affectionate nickname "The Bodger." Bodger means anyone who creates something (including art) from a mashup of improvized and found objects. Many of his shows succeeded and many did not, but all took big creative risks.

As the conversation continued, I suspected Bogdanov was taunting each of us to find another layer of meaning in his comment. To me, he was saying that preparation, intellectual rigor and obsessive commitment only went so far. Directing also needs a portion of Plato's "divine madness." To become an artist, a director must also be able to access the wild, irreverent, imaginative, loving, ridiculous, and unconventional impulses within. Managing that contradictory combination of "committed, disciplined, and logical preparation" and "creative, illogical, and magic fire of inspiration" is at the center of any director's journey.

This book is designed to help you find your best practices for directing in the professional theatre, and so enable you to achieve your own artistic vision. It aims to give you practical guidance, while also acknowledging the aspirational and visionary.

If you are passionately committed to direct and aspire to a professional career as a master storyteller, read on. If you find special, unmatched fulfillment in the artistry of live theatre, with its collaborative process, its multiple creative tasks, its transformative powers, and its potential to astonish and reveal the human condition, read on. If you are captivated by that moment when the lights dim and the ritual of theatre comes to life, read on. If you long for the experience when audience and artists become one, read on.

"In the theatre, everyone wants to direct!" Like many a backstage comment, this outburst by a frustrated director is an exaggeration. Many aspire to be a director. Many do not. At first glance, directing appears to be an intoxicating blend of artistry, power, and prestige. Borrowing the mystique of the cinema, the role of theatre director occasionally has been elevated to "auteur"; in other words, a single master artist who uses every source, including the script, the actors, the designers, and anything from another arts discipline to create a dazzlingly innovative theatrical experience. However, this version of the genius artist/autocrat actually belies the collaborative nature of theatre. Perhaps the term "visionary director" is more useful. In the century or so since directing became a profession, visionary directors have created revelatory productions and advanced the entire art form. Although better known for his system of actor training, Konstantin Stanislavski is recognized as a pioneer in developing the idea of the "theatre director." His pursuit of "realism" and insistence on "believable" human beings on stage profoundly changed the director's work for generations. Although better known today for his plays, Bertolt Brecht developed an entirely new dramatic form: The Epic Theatre, based upon the *Verfremdungseffekt* (commonly translated as the distancing or alienation effect), which transformed the director's work. He refused to let the audience psychologically identify with any character, because he believed that empathy encouraged sentimental, emotionally indulgent escapism; rather, he wanted to startle and provoke the audience into critical thinking. Both these visionary artists profoundly changed our understanding of theatrical performance. And they both chose to do so by creating companies of artists and craftspeople.

Peter Brook, the author of *The Empty Space,* is widely considered the most influential and innovative director working during the past 50 years. Brook established his reputation at the Royal Shakespeare Company by staging innovative productions of classics and new plays, such as *Marat/Sade* and his groundbreaking "white box" production of *A Midsummer Night's Dream.* After leaving the RSC, Brook went on to found the International Centre for Theatre Research in Paris, a multi-national company of artists. He explored the enduring myths of international cultures, and reinvented the way plays and theatrical events are created and staged. He toured worldwide, presenting international productions such as *The Mahabharata* based upon a Sanskrit epic. His theories, writings, and productions have changed the professional theatre around the world and have influenced multiple generations of directors. Such visionary directors are invaluable to theatre, the arts, and fellow artists; they expand our understanding of theatre and the world around us. However, truth be told, few of us possess the genius to reimagine and reinvent the art form.

In today's professional theatre, the director is most commonly considered to be the leading artistic interpreter of a theatrical work created by another principal artist, such as the playwright or the musical team of composer, lyricist, and book writer. However, this view of the director's role as storyteller has not limited directors to conventional means of telling theatrical stories. Harold Prince was a prolific Broadway producer who directed the premieres of Stephen Sondheim's musicals with a theatrical boldness and vision that matched the creative impulses of their composer. In recent years, the Scottish director John Doyle has radically reimagined the staging and interpretation of Sondheim's musicals. The Belgian director Ivo van Hove has received international acclaim for his radical and fresh approach to the plays of Arthur Miller, breaking from the realism of Miller's original director, the celebrated Elia Kazan. All these directors staged stories in innovative, imaginative, and astonishing ways, but the scripts and scores came from others.

At any level of our industry, you will hear mythic stories of productions that experienced agonizing deaths at the hands of the director. These "terrible directors" create concepts that undermine the script instead of illuminating it. They don't know what they want, they don't know how to talk to actors, and they don't care about anyone else's ideas or contributions. Their arrogance and egoism leads to outbursts of temper or lacerating criticism. On the other hand, you will hear that "brilliant directors" intuitively know when to give actors direction and when to leave them alone. They are exceptionally inspirational, collaborative, and gifted leaders who can solve the most difficult or challenging scenes, while appreciating everyone's ideas and contributions. They know what they want in tech, and they never try to redirect the play in previews. If these expectations sound extreme, they are! But they also reveal the primacy and power of the director in today's theatre, as well as a deep hunger for inspired, skilled, and deft direction. And they expose a deep anxiety about being trapped or caught in a failing production. These terrible and brilliant extremes point out a hard truth about directing: our work can damn a production to mediocrity or worse, but it can also lift a show to brilliance and occasionally to transcendence.

The task of learning how to direct (or direct better) can be confusing when we examine the radically different approaches adopted by many accomplished directors. One director controls every possible beat or gesture, choreographing in detail the physical life of each actor's performance, while another waits for the actors to instinctively figure out the blocking before stepping in. One director focuses on the text, verse, and rhetoric, obsessed with the flow of thought and emotion through the "sound and delivery" of the actor's voice, while another takes the same script and focuses on the raw emotion and psychological authenticity in the acting. Some directors dictate to designers the visual world they want, while others want and need the designers' ideas to find the best conceptual solution. Some directors use improvization, theatre games, and exercises based upon group therapy while others stick to traditional rehearsal techniques. Some never change their rehearsal/production approach (e.g., every show follows the same series of steps), while others change their practice of rehearsal/production with each new project. Each of these methods may succeed. The trick is to find out what combination of approaches works best for you.

Each of us is drawn to directing for many reasons. All directors want to create a visually thrilling, emotionally engaging, thought-provoking, and revelatory production. At the same time, each of us is influenced by what we believe the purpose of theatre should be today. Is it "holding the mirror up to nature" or providing dazzling and diverting entertainment? Is it the pursuit of social justice and political change or a means of creating cross-cultural understanding, empathy, and tolerance?

And what about our personal beliefs: Does the theatre need a radical reappraisal? A revolution? Or should the traditional practices be protected and nurtured? You may and should ask yourself what is at the root of your attraction to the art. I have often thought that part of my attraction to the job is rooted in the director's task of staging and managing conflicts, which

I could not do as a child. Whatever our reasons, a director must lead; in the end, it is our responsibility to stand up and captain the ship.

For the beginning director, the objectives may be more aspirational, ideological, and ambitious than practical. This book has no intention of squelching the ambitions of a young director. The theatre field constantly needs passion, new ideas, and fresh perspective. Indeed, a grand vision of becoming a master director who advances the theatrical field (and changes the world) with boldly reimagined, revolutionary productions is laudable. However, to achieve that level of artistic impact, the inventiveness and vitality of your directorial vision must be matched by the highest level of skill, expertise, and professionalism that you can attain.

Art, craft, and business

The premise of this book is straightforward. I believe that professional directing requires expertise in these three areas. **Art** acknowledges that the evolution of an artist takes a lifetime and, since this is a public and collaborative art, encompasses far more than simply developing your own personal aesthetic. Your mastery of the art and aesthetic will be built by directing and directing and directing and directing. In the beginning, you must proactively find the work or produce it for yourself at any level possible. Although learning to work as an entrepreneur will prove an invaluable skill throughout your career, it's most important to develop an imaginative, thoughtful and inspiring artistic vision, based upon your personal aesthetic and point-of-view. Your vision must attract collaborators and colleagues. To do so, you must first foster a deep understanding of human relations and psychology to develop the art of persuasion. You will need agile and adept people skills to attract a host of collaborators and contributors who will help you create thrilling, engaging, and revelatory performances. As your circle of fellow artists expands, you will also find mentors who can push you, challenge you, and help you advance your artistic vision and your career.

You will especially need to understand actors, love and respect their remarkable gifts and their unique ability to perform eight times a week, baring their souls to each audience. If you dislike actors, don't direct. You should also strive to create long-term relationships with playwrights and musical teams (e.g., composers, lyricists, and book writers). These are the theatre's foundational artists—without their work, you don't have anything to direct. Find and meet designers, composers, and other artists who will help you craft your vision. And remember to find, meet, and develop relationships with producers and artistic directors, because they hire you.

Forging your artistry as a director demands a lively imagination as well as courage, persuasive leadership talents, and ongoing curiosity about the many other art forms and crafts that contribute to the performance. All this requires a sophisticated and thorough education in the theatre itself. I can't stress enough the importance of seeing theatre in performance; see as much as you possibly can. It is vital. It is also critical that you read as many plays as you can. You should also cultivate an insatiable hunger for learning the stories of past cultures, but also keeping current with the most urgent issues in the world today.

At the same time, you must keep abreast of the state of the field, know what's being produced, and be aware of current innovations and trends, such as radical experiments in actor/audience relationship (e.g., productions that immerse audiences in a 360-degree environment) or industry-wide initiatives to increase equity, diversity, and inclusion of women and artists of color. All this will inform the development of your aesthetic.

Craft relates to the skills, techniques, and disciplines required to get from the first rehearsal to opening night. For the director, the list can be very long: knowledge of language, voice and dialect; techniques and tools for team building, collaboration, and engagement; management skills to lead people with disparate personalities, experiences, habits, and jobs. In addition, you'll need to improve your expertise in script analysis; train your ear in music; learn to visualize a set from a ground plan with or without a model or sketches; and develop and refine your visual and spatial awareness to increase your kinetic knowledge of the human body in space and time. Having a specific understanding of, and demonstrating your appreciation for, the work of individual production shops and staffs can profoundly affect the success of a production. For example, let's consider Stephen Sondheim's masterwork, *Sweeney Todd: The Demon Barber of Fleet Street*. The design, mechanism, safety, and efficiency of the barber chair and its "dead body" drop chute is critical to the success of the musical and affects the acting and staging. Sweeney must cut the throats of two "clients" while singing the lovely, romantic ballad of "Johanna" with the young male lead, Anthony, in Act II. Completing this complicated physical action smoothly without interrupting the singing is paramount. No doubt the scene designer will have proposed solutions, but a director's positive working relationship with the production staff will do much to ensure a successful technical rehearsal. Actively engage the entire team in creating and troubleshooting the chair. If you've motivated your cast, crew, and shops properly, the head of props, technical director, stage manager, crew members, and fight and movement director will work closely with the actor playing Sweeney, to find the best solution that works safely and reliably night after night. Indeed, building a positive working relationship with the technical director and prop master is a smart practice for any production.

Business considerations in this book are not about the "commerce of theatre" (i.e., understanding financial statements or marketing plans), but rather focus on professional practices in the field including joining unions; negotiating contracts; working with agents, managers, artistic directors, and producers; creating and maintaining a network of colleagues and advocates. As a freelance director, not only do you need to understand the typical steps in being interviewed and hired, but you also need to develop a method to evaluate and then wisely use the resources and capabilities of each theatre that hires you. In some instances, you may need to "self-produce" the production. In theatres with adequate resources and staffing, the artistic and production staffs will take care of producing the show. However, in theatres with limited resources, overworked staffs, or poor leadership, your artistic vision will almost certainly fail unless you actively marshal the entire organization to be part of your team. The most effective way of doing this is to authentically engage the staff by inspiring them, showing appreciation of their work, checking in frequently and including them in the process. By doing so, you can turn even the most burned-out administrator or overworked craftsperson into an excited, inspired collaborator.

Business topics will also include an examination of the differences between freelance directing and artistic direction, the job duties of artistic directors, common organizational governance structures, and tips for seeking and securing this leadership.

For the purposes of this book, let me define my use of the term "professional." I use the term more narrowly to keep this book to a manageable and useful length. For the purposes of this book, a "professional director" is a member of the directors' union who works a significant portion of the year at his or her chosen profession. A "professional theatre" is defined as a subsidized (UK) or not-for-profit organization (US), and one that hires a significant portion of their performers from the actors' union, has full-time leadership, and operates with sufficient human and financial resources. My background leans towards professional companies capable of producing fully realized productions and performances. In the commercial theatre, the term "professional" applies to for-profit producers and organizations that produce and/or present productions on Broadway, the West End, No. 1 Tours, or at other for-profit venues, such as dinner theatres, and who hire union-affiliated actors, directors, choreographers, designers, musicians, etc.

To train or not to train

Over the past 30 years, the training of directors has become far more comprehensive and sophisticated. The number of new director training programs established on both sides of the Atlantic has increased substantially. Studios, universities, and conservatories now offer certificates, undergraduate, and graduate degrees in directing. In the US, a Master of Fine Arts (MFA) in directing has almost become a prerequisite for early employment in the profession. In the UK, the pathway of training and then entering the professional theatre is more defined. Although many universities now offer an MFA or Masters (MA) in directing, many directors also graduate with academic degrees and then follow established early career pathways to directing, such as apprenticing or serving as an assistant director, before moving into directing.

The first step in deciding whether you need formal training is to evaluate the depth and breadth of your knowledge and experience in directing. Then you should evaluate the quality of training you would receive, alongside the potential advantages and disadvantages in earning a degree from a specific institution. There are several benefits and advantages to attending a strong training program for directors:

- thorough and detailed education in the art, theories, and methodologies of contemporary directing;
- multiple opportunities to direct projects and productions;
- a gifted, engaging, and experienced faculty, some of whom are also working professionals;
- exposure to dramatic literature (from international classics to new plays), and the history, evolution, and practice of stage direction. Several programs also include a review of the social, cultural, political, and economic ideas and forces that have influenced or been influenced by the theatre;

- development of your personal aesthetic as a director;
- industry reputation of the program, based upon the success and influence of its graduates and faculty;
- widespread access to, and connections in, the professional field;
- close relationship with a professional theatre;
- exploration and understanding of the associated fields of acting, design, and playwriting, etc.;
- geographic location near a major city that offers a wide array of professional theatre;
- development of a personal network.

To be sure, few programs offer all these benefits. Some offer only a few. Based upon the belief that a director needs a strong foundation in performance, some programs require their directing students to join the acting course for a year or more before moving full-time into director training. In addition, several programs (perhaps recognizing the difficulty of a career in the professional theatre) have a split goal of training you both to direct and to teach. Because this book focuses on directing rather than teaching, I don't recommend training programs that primarily concentrate on an academic approach to directing with little or no reference to the profession. In the US, formal training can come at a high cost and you should consider this carefully before reaching any decision. Graduating with a debt of $50,000 to $250,000 in student loans can cripple your chances to pursue a full-time career in theatre. A few programs offer full scholarships and a stipend for living expenses. Many offer partial scholarship or financial aid. To reduce the cost of training, post-graduate students often must take on significant teaching roles as part of a graduate assistantship. Examine carefully the average number of opportunities each directing student is given during the full course of training. Are these class projects or fully produced productions? Also check the admission rates for programs. Schools typically admit a handful of directing students each year, and the most competitive schools attract large numbers of highly qualified and experienced candidates. A colleague of mine who heads an MFA directing program on the West Coast told me that the most recent admissions process considered 88 candidates for 2 places. That said, there are several remarkable programs in both countries that offer excellent training, and remarkable access to the theatre field. These programs often have a lasting effect on your growth as an artist and as a professional.

The sharp increase in training programs implies that directing for the professional theatre is a high demand occupation on both sides of the

Atlantic. Sadly, it's not. In the past 50 years, the growth of the subsidized or not-for-profit companies (regional, repertory, or resident theatres), and the proliferation of ensembles and emergent companies in regional cities increased the opportunities for gifted, well-trained, effective, and imaginative directors. However, the past decade has seen a reversal in the trend; several not-for-profit theatres in the US have closed. The increasing economic risks of producing in commercial theatre or in large institutional theatres often push their leaders to stress financial rather than artistic success simply to stay in business. This in turn puts pressure upon the freelance director to deliver an economically as well as an artistically successful production, no matter what. Regrettably, this "market pressure" leads many theatres to repeatedly hire from the same group of familiar, experienced directors. To break through this system, you need to be prepared to direct a wide variety of shows. You should become equally adept at directing a spectacular, popular musical on a large stage and a provocative new play on a small stage. Although you may strongly prefer intense tragedies or cutting-edge new plays, you may be employed and become known for directing contemporary comedies.

The obstacles and challenges to enter and then to advance in the profession were similar when I began my career. However, the theatre field was undergoing an expansion across North America. Today's theatre is very different. The technological revolution has brought unexpected competition for theatres across the world in the form of personal entertainment devices. Although the internet and the smart phone have profoundly changed the way we communicate, they have also undermined deeper, authentic connections between people and cultures. Our personal devices promised infinite information, entertainment choices, and instantaneous, interpersonal communication for all; but also they deprived us of the extended live and personal interactions and conversations that we need to survive as humans. I believe this creates an extraordinary opportunity for the "live ritual" of theatre.

In both the US and the UK, the past decade has seen significant increases in the development and production of new plays and musicals, opportunities for diverse and/or female voices and leaders, and interest in new experiments in cross-disciplinary and interactive theatre. Theatre in the US is also undergoing an enormous generational change in artistic directors. These transitions provide extraordinary opportunities. Directors can and should lead the field by creating performances that will attract new artists and audiences to the "live theatre" by re-imagining the possibilities of theatrical performance while nurturing the enduring traditions of theatre. Directors will be needed to lead the field and advance the relevance, value, and transformative power of live theatre.

My life has been greatly enriched and I have been deeply fulfilled by my work in the professional theatre. Directing so many theatrical stories has helped me understand my place in the world as well as revealed the lives of the many peoples, cultures, and communities other than mine. Each play brings new challenges, but also provides the exhilarating opportunity to explore and learn new facts and ideas about my fellow humans. There is an enormous satisfaction in directing an ensemble of artists to open a "window on the world" and this inspires me to continue. What I have learned from my own career as a freelance director and then artistic director has given me much to pass along to beginning and emerging directors as well as to those who are contemplating leading a theatre. You will almost certainly face hardships as a professional director, but you can succeed, too, with hard work, spirit, and artistry.

Directing Professionally is a combination of practical advice and aesthetic exploration. I hope to strike a balance between the artistic, intellectual, social, and cultural roles of a director and the working realities of professional theatre today. Throughout the book, I will include observations, comments, and tips from myself and other professionals who have succeeded as freelance directors and/or artistic/producing leaders. The book will cover four periods in a director's career: (1) entering the profession and finding a pathway to directing, (2) navigating and succeeding at your first professional directing job, (3) advancing your professional career and artistry to garner regular employment at theatres that pay a living wage, and (4) evaluating whether to become an artistic director or not.

Part I, "Entering the Theatre Field," describes the training, leadership skills, artistic vision, knowledge and expertise you will need to become a professional director in either the not-for-profit/subsidized theatres or in the commercial theatre. It guides you in refining and focusing your first career goals and describes common entry points for an early career artist. In addition to exploring associated jobs, Part I lays out several routes to professional direction and suggests ways to find mentors and advocates who can educate you as well as advance your career. This part covers the directors' unions; negotiating contracts; working with agents, artistic directors, and producers; creating and maintaining a network of colleagues and advocates; undertaking self-promotion; and handling messages and communications. It also addresses surviving and thriving as a person as you build your resumé.

When your needs and aspirations are added to your personal and financial needs (e.g., maintaining long-distance relationships, having a family and/or a home, health insurance, etc.), you may find that you will require additional sources of income to support your career. Anyone who works in theatre must face this economic challenge, but it is particularly difficult for freelance artists, including directors. Fortunately, there are several opportunities within theatre (e.g., artistic associate, resident director, associate artistic director) and dozens of jobs outside the field that require the leadership and creative talents of a professional director.

Part II, "Your First Professional Job," jumps ahead to another key moment in your career. That is, directing in the professional theatre for the first time. *Directing Professionally* will not teach you the fundamentals of direction (there are many excellent books for that); instead, it presumes you possess the necessary training and experience. Rather than a theoretical approach, it will adopt a pragmatic one, from the point of being seriously considered to direct a play or musical at a mid-size or larger professional theatre, to being interviewed and then hired. It will refer to the many skills and practices that you learned in your training and discuss pre-production tasks such as casting and working with your creative team of designers from the viewpoint of a director and an artistic director. This part will lay out the professional process of directing from first rehearsal through opening night, including advice on table work, staging, scene work, tech, dress and previews, openings and audience and critical response.

Part III, "Advancing Your Career," proposes ways in which you can expand the impact, recognition, and reputation of your work as a director in the professional theatre. The most significant challenge for any freelance director is to work regularly. The occasional job can be very exciting and fulfilling, but you need to earn a living as you improve your artistry and build your resume. How can you move from an occasional freelance gig to multiple, regular gigs at multiple theatres? More importantly, how can you move from small theatres with limited resources and little field exposure to larger theatres with greater resources and wider exposure? This section includes tips and techniques to leverage your growing network of artists, artistic directors, managing directors, producers, media, and industry contacts to support your artistry and career. It also suggests how to expand your directorial repertoire.

The final section, Part IV, "Becoming an Artistic Director," examines the role and the common responsibilities and duties of an artistic director in the subsidized or not-for-profit theatre. It lays out the typical recruitment process and lists the range of topics and questions that you may be asked by recruiters, trustees or governors, current staff, and even donors. This part will give you a sense of the exciting but often challenging transition from freelance directing to artistic directing an organization with multiple productions and projects. It will explore the current conditions of the field, and the expectations placed upon artistic directors. For example, artistic directors today are not only expected to provide artistic leadership, but also to work effectively on fundraising, trustee relationships, people management, scheduling and budgeting, strategic planning, financial stewardship, and more. Part IV is intended to help you make an informed choice when deciding whether you want to pursue institutional leadership or not. This part concludes with information and advice for those beginning the job, including how to build strong relationships with trustees, managing/executive directors, as well as artistic and management staffs, and articulating and achieving your vision as an artistic director, while continuing to practice your primary passion of directing.

Directing Professionally draws upon my experience of 30+ years in hiring dozens of freelance directors for every imaginable project, from Shakespearean tragedies to cutting-edge world premieres, from book musicals to "ensemble-created" events. From that perspective, I hope to assist you in launching and advancing your career as a professional theatre director.

Part I

Entering the Theatre Field

1

The Big Leap

Graduating with a degree in directing is both exhilarating and terrifying. You're ready to direct, but anxieties immediately crowd in: Where is my first job? How do I break into the world of professional directing with my training? How can I possibly earn a living in theatre? Before letting these legitimate concerns overwhelm you, take time to figure out what you want to do and where you want to live.

The late Michael Langham (Artistic Director of The Birmingham Rep, The Stratford Festival in Canada, and The Guthrie Theatre) taught me the valuable lifelong practice of "answering the why." Why do you want to direct in the theatre? This question immediately led to two others: What do you want to direct? And why? To start, answer these questions:

1 What do you want to direct? Be specific. Which plays? What genres or styles? For instance, are you drawn to the satiric comedies of Molière

or to hard-hitting, dark, and edgy new plays? Are you interested in directing traditional musicals or in creating immersive and interactive experiences? What plays do you believe are most relevant and powerful in today's world? Are you drawn to theatrical works or events that seek to address injustices, such as inequality for women, or systemic racism? Prioritize your list to those ideas that stimulate you most as a director. Narrow the list again.

2 Next, research and compile a list of directors who focus on those titles or that kind of work. If you love musicals in a commercial setting, find out the directors of your favorite titles. If a new play captures your interest, find out the playwright and the director. If you love European or American classics, look for directors who regularly succeed with these plays. For each genre, there are many successful and talented directors. Narrow the list to a manageable size by considering your own directorial style and approach. For instance, are you driven to create innovative or provocative productions of Shakespeare with diverse or gender fluid casting? Or is your directing of Shakespeare more focused on the acting and the text? Do you want to explore "Original Practice"? Research the directors who match your aesthetic and find out where they live and work. And then note the theatres and producing organizations that hire them regularly.

3 Finally, look at the companies that focus on the titles, kind of work, and artistic approach you prefer. Which producer brought your favorite musicals to Broadway or the West End? Which theatres commissioned, developed, and/or premiered your favorite new plays? Examine each organization's commitment to this specific genre, its long-term achievement, its impact on the field, and its size and resources.

Review your three lists. Look for patterns and overlaps. Reflecting upon these lists will help you not only develop your personal aesthetic, but also define your early career goals. This exercise will also aid you with the next big decision—where to live and pursue work.

Location, location, location

Where you choose to live should mirror the type and kind of work you most want to pursue. That location should have multiple opportunities to pursue work inside and outside the theatre, to learn about the field, and to grow as an artist and a professional. Consider your personal needs alongside your professional aspirations. Work out the cost of living and quality of lifestyle that you can afford and accept. Many recent graduates immediately move to London or New York, the two indisputable "centers of professional theatre." These cities are exciting, invigorating, and stimulating, because each has an unmatched number of theatres, performances, and fellow artists. However, they are also very expensive and intensely competitive. If you've been fortunate to attend one of the top-tier training programs in or around these cities, you may have easier access to theatre jobs. However, most theatre artists discover that it typically takes three to five years to build the necessary connections, experience and reputation to garner regular employment in the professional theatre in these cities.

Other early career directors choose cities other than New York or London that have thriving theatre scenes. In the United States, Chicago leads the pack with more than 240 theatre companies, but there are many other cities, including Minneapolis, Seattle, Los Angeles (and Southern California), Houston, Atlanta, San Francisco, Washington DC, and Boston. In the UK, thriving theatre cities include Manchester, Glasgow, Cardiff, Sheffield, Edinburgh, and Birmingham.

Some directors will choose a specific place to live and work based upon personal or family preference. Others make a choice based upon the mission of a particular company. For instance, the Pentabus Theatre Company in Bromfield, Shropshire, a rural theatre company whose mission "is [to] tour new plays to village halls, fields, and theatres across the country, telling stories with local relevance and national impact."[1] The mission of Junebug Productions in New Orleans is "to create and support artistic works that question and confront inequitable conditions that have historically impacted the African-American community. Through interrogation, we challenge ourselves and those aligned with the organization to make greater and deeper contributions towards a just society."[2]

Keep in mind that choosing where to live and work is an important decision, but probably not a permanent one. Most theatre people will live and work in many different places throughout their careers.

Money, money, money

The next big issue is income—after all, you need to make enough to live. We all hope to immediately find work in theatre, but often the reality is that we need a survival job. Look for the following:

1 Entry-level jobs in mid-size or large theatre companies, with an emphasis on the artistic, literary, stage management, production, and arts education departments. One of my colleagues worked for a few years in the literary department at a New York theatre acclaimed for producing new plays. He read hundreds of new plays. As he was given more responsibilities, he met and worked with dozens of playwrights. When he returned to his directing career, he immediately began directing world premieres of new plays because of his extensive network as a literary associate.

2 Unrelated or part-time jobs in professional theatres that gain you access to shows, staff, and experience. If you have skills in carpentry, graphics, house management, and more, use those to get a job—especially in a theatre that produces work you admire.

3 Teaching and/or coaching. Many theatre artists begin their careers by teaching acting or directing at secondary schools for the performing arts, or at universities, conservatories, and studios. Teaching is challenging work, and it often brings more rigor to our directing, because it demands that we must practice what we teach. Some directors become accomplished as acting coaches and work with many levels of actors. Others create studios that specialize in specific parts of the profession, such as preparation and techniques for auditioning.

4 Entry-level jobs in a related part of the industry, such as an assistant to a casting director, agent or personal manager, a general manager in the commercial theatre, or a staff member at a theatrical media and marketing firm, etc.

5 Non-theatre jobs that both pay well and provide flexibility to pursue your directing career. These include the stereotypical jobs of bartending or waiting tables. However, a director's managerial skills can also give you opportunities to manage restaurants or offices, serve as a sales person, work as personal assistant to a celebrity, plan and execute corporate events or not-for-profit galas, coordinate production calendars at media companies, or pursue other creative tasks such as website design, graphic design, videography and photography, and many more. After moving to New York City to pursue directing, I worked as a temp, typing into computers large volumes of pro-forma press releases, correspondence, manuals, and media announcements. When I became frustrated with the bland and awkward writing, I started editing and revising the content. Rather than being fired, I was

then promoted several times, eventually working as a writer of speeches, confidential correspondence, and strategic plans for the CEO of a multi-national corporation. That experience also taught me much about good and bad leadership.

Developing your aesthetic

The process of finding and developing your personal aesthetic and your artistic voice and vision will take many years. At the beginning of your career, you will have been heavily influenced by your faculty mentors and your university or conservatory program. You will also have your own dreams, aspirations, and ambitions for your career as a director.

My best advice to any young director is two-fold: **See as much theatre as you can! Read as much about theatre as you can!** When I trained at London's Guildhall School of Music & Drama, my scholarship was so generous that I was able to see more than 200 shows in three years. Although I was blessed with brilliant, field-leading teachers and artists from the Royal Shakespeare Company (e.g., Cicely Berry), attending so many productions turned out to be the most important part of my education as a director. Seeing professional theatre is especially valuable, but don't limit yourself— see everything, from the Fringe to the West End. Attend scruffy, upstart companies with little money but big ideas, and university productions of plays you've always wanted to see. Look at Off-Off Broadway and regional ensemble theatres, and attend public readings of new plays or musicals. The point is simple—you can find inspiration, artistic ideas, and even future colleagues anywhere and at any level. Also, see the types of plays or interactive shows that expand your understanding of theatrical performance. And make a point of seeing the plays and genres that you think you "hate."

Going to the theatre can be exorbitantly expensive. But there's no need to pay full price. Ask a friend or colleague for a comp ticket, take advantage of any free performances, or buy reduced-price tickets via community outreach programs. Many theatres now offer free or low-price tickets to attract young adults, via "student rush" day-of-show ticket lotteries and "Under 30" programs. In addition, there are several discount ticket offers on theatre media sites online and through various apps. In New York, the not-for-profit Theatre Development Fund offers reduced-price tickets to musicals and plays at its TKTS booths;[3] in London, the Society of London Theatres offers reduced-price tickets to several West End shows at its Leicester Square

TKTS kiosk.[4] Many regional theatres and cities have adopted their own version of these services, selling heavily discounted tickets to local or regional theatre shows. In the UK, several theatres offer "day seats," which are released at a set time on the morning of the performance. Check other theatre websites for special programs, such as the 10p tickets at the Royal Court Theatre or the Travelex season at the National Theatre, when more than half the tickets are offered for £15.

Also, don't forget that you can see shows by volunteering or working as an usher or in front-of-house staff. The acclaimed Artistic Director of Hong Kong Repertory Theatre, Anthony Chan, has had a prolific career in directing, playwriting, and the training of directors. During and after his undergraduate and graduate education at the University of Colorado, Chan served as a volunteer usher at the Denver Center for the Performing (the parent organization of the Theatre Company which I led). Ushering gave Chan the opportunity to see as many as 40 shows a year, from Broadway tours to regional theatre productions, at no cost. He counts watching these performances as one of the most valuable parts of his director training.

If you live in a smaller or regional community with less access to professional theatre, there are an increasing number of live or taped live broadcasts of stage productions from The National Theatre, Royal Shakespeare Company, Kenneth Branagh Theatre Company, and Bridge Theatre (UK); Live from Lincoln Center, PBS's Great Performances Series, and Fathom Events (US), and several companies via Stage Russia, including Satirikon Theatre, Lensoviet Theatre, Stanislavski Electro Theatre, Theatre Art Studio, and Vakhtangov Theatre.[5] Finally, in New York City, you can make an appointment to watch onsite video recordings of many past Broadway and regional productions at the New York Public Library for the Performing Arts at Lincoln Center.[6]

Your second task is to **read as much about theatre as you can.** Read plays and read/listen to musicals, but also explore screenplays, adaptations, and revised editions. Read anything about the plays that most interest you, including their topics, time periods, original productions, and the background of the playwright. Read theatrical biographies and autobiographies, interviews, blogs, magazines, and newspapers. Then widen your reading to include social, cultural, political and historical, economic, religious, and philosophical commentaries. Visit the theatre and/or performing arts collections and exhibits at museums: check the collections at the Victoria and Albert Museum;[7] the permanent exhibition at the Globe Theatre;[8] the Theatre Museum of New York;[9] and various regional museums, including the

Burlesque Hall of Fame in Las Vegas, Nevada; or the Wick Theatre and Costume Museum in Boca Raton, Florida. Then expand your visits to exhibits, collections, and museums in any of the visual and performing arts.

Finding a pathway forward

As you define your aesthetic, you will be working to establish your career. There are many jobs and experiences that lead to professional directing. Some of these are:

1 **Assist experienced directors.** This provides invaluable opportunities to observe several directors in action as they mount productions working with professional actors, designers, etc. You can observe the styles, conceptual ideas, artistic choices, practices, tools and techniques that succeed, as well as those that fail. Another benefit of assistant directing is expanding your professional contacts. In the US, a handful of theatres have formal internship or apprentice positions, although many are not focused specifically upon directing. Several opportunities are associated with specific MFA training programs. Few pay a livable wage, but some provide a small weekly stipend or housing. Early and mid-career directors can apply to Stage Directors and Choreographers Foundation or SDCF (the charitable foundation associated with the director's union) for grants to observe master directors throughout the rehearsal of a production. In the UK, there are assistant directing positions at several subsidized theatres, supported by local Arts Councils or industries. In addition, there are organizations serving professional development for new and emerging theatre directors, such as the Regional Theatre Young Directors Scheme.[10]

2 **Don't wait. Start your own company, and direct what you want.** It doesn't matter how tiny it is. Create an ensemble or join one. This provides you with multiple opportunities to direct, experiment, learn your craft, and hopefully draw attention to your talent. Although it's hard work and risky, founding a company also teaches you about the multiple and necessary tasks that you must undertake to produce (e.g., finding rehearsal and performance spaces; attracting fellow artists to commit to the work; and begging, borrowing, and stealing props, costumes, set materials, and even theatre seats). For inspiration, research the history of Steppenwolf Theatre in Chicago. Or Icarus

Theatre Collective in the UK, whose artistic policy states "Icarus creates theatre that is kinetic, intellectual, and visceral: Theatre that moves. We choose to relish what others shy away from, show what others daren't; destroy boundaries when others would create rules. We explore the beauty of the text and skill of the actor to consider harsh, brutal themes with a modern examination of Theatre of the Absurd in classic and contemporary storytelling."[11]

3 **Become the entrepreneur of your own career.** Produce your own shows. Several of the entrepreneur's skills and tasks will prove very useful to any director, including raising and managing money, building relationships with an ever-evolving list of advocates and industry contacts, managing people (volunteers, artists and staff), running scenarios to explore different ways of reaching your goals, creating effective social media, dealing with failure, and even improving the world.

4 **Direct workshops and readings of new plays or musicals.** Work with early career playwrights or teams of composers, lyricists, and book writers (perhaps your former classmates?). These developmental activities are typically supported by theatres and producing organizations with formal new works programs, and they have greatly increased over the past two decades. Now dozens of theatres commission and/or develop scripts through workshops and public readings and premieres, often producing annual festivals to showcase the new work. Major festivals include: The Humana Festival (Actor's Theatre of Louisville), Pacific Playwright's Festival (South Coast Rep), Colorado New Play Summit (Denver Center Theatre Company). Several not-for-profit organizations support playwrights with residencies, office space, workshops, and readings for any project, but do not produce. These include New York's New Dramatists[12] and Lark Theatre Company,[13] Minneapolis' Playwright's Center,[14] and Connecticut's Eugene O'Neill Theater Center.[15]

5 **Direct anywhere and everywhere**: small companies, ensembles, academic organizations, semi-professional theatres, and even amateur theatres (in the US, called "community theatres" (Association of American Association of Community Theatres), but in the UK, called "amateur theatres" (AmDram)). Although many amateur companies only use volunteer artists, others are more sophisticated, hiring professional directors, designers, and occasionally actors. Directing for theatres of many different sizes, resources, and levels of professionalism

can improve your directing skills and increase your capacity to adapt. And sometimes these activities will add to your resumé and provide additional income.

Leverage your faculty and fellow alumni

The most effective help to transitioning from training programs to professional theatre (and a new city) often comes from the faculty and alumni of your university or conservatory. If faculty members of your training program included professional directors, they are often willing to connect you to jobs and opportunities (including serving as an assistant on their productions). Several prestigious conservatories and universities increase the access to jobs and agents for their graduates. Given its remarkable record in graduating accomplished and significant artists and leaders over the past 80+ years, graduates of the Yale School of Drama are referred to as the "Yale Mafia," a backhanded compliment, prompted by envy but also admiration of the greater prestige, opportunity, and success enjoyed by the school's alumni. A similar prestige is enjoyed by "Oxbridge" graduates in the UK. The term refers to graduates of Oxford and Cambridge Universities, who are often chosen early to direct professionally or to lead companies. However, a degree from any of these well-known conservatories or universities doesn't guarantee a successful career. You have to deliver when given the opportunity.

In reality, the list of prestigious programs is much, much longer, including The Juilliard School, New York University, Northwestern University, University of California/Irvine, Columbia University, DePaul Theatre School, University of California/San Diego, Boston University, University of Washington, and more. In the UK, Royal Academy of Dramatic Arts, Guildhall School of Music and Drama, The Royal Central School of Speech and Drama, London Academy of Music and Dramatic Arts, Universities of Leicester, Bristol, and Exeter, as well as conservatories at Glasgow's Citizens Theatre and, in Ireland, Dublin's Abbey Theatre, among others. Each of these has highly successful graduates and active alumni groups that can provide access, useful information and advice.

If you have not graduated from a well-known institution, don't despair. Many directors graduate from other programs across the UK and US and find success in the field. Our industry is constantly looking for new and innovative artists regardless of their degree. Neither the College of William & Mary nor the Guildhall School of Drama offered programs or degrees in directing. My journey to a directing career was a continual process of self-education, learning by doing and doing, interspersed with moments of good luck.

Understanding professional expectations

It's useful to know what is expected of a professional director in different sectors of the field. Artistic directors and commercial producers expect the best show possible. Given the ever-increasing human and financial resources required to mount a show and/or operate a company, artistic directors expect you to achieve a measure of box office as well as artistic success. As a master storyteller, the professional director is responsible for creating a dynamic, stirring, and relevant directorial concept and interpretation of the play; charting the best route to achieve that vision; and leading everyone to the best possible performance, all **within** the resources provided by the producer or the theatre.

In order to clarify expectations, let's examine the differing missions, motives, working environments and goals of theatre by looking at (1) your training program, (2) not-for-profit/subsidized theatres, (3) the commercial theatre (Broadway, the West End, national tours, dinner theatres, etc.), and (4) universities and conservatories. During training, your university or conservatory program was appropriately focused on you as a student, providing an education and mentorship so that you could earn a degree in theatre directing. Without a doubt, the faculty wanted your education to be enlightening and inspiring. They enabled you to develop your personal aesthetic and talents by providing you with the knowledge, skills, and experiences that you needed to direct after graduation. However, you were the student and they were the experts. Their influence upon you was enormous. After all, they graded you and determined exactly what you had to do to earn that degree. If your theatre program included student actors, designers, playwrights, and production technicians, directing a production became very complicated. The head of acting rarely has the same goals as the heads of directing, scenic design, or playwriting. Understandably, each teacher has her own talents, aesthetic viewpoint, expertise in and opinions about her professional specialty, and each has differing beliefs about the social, cultural, political, and artistic role of theatre in contemporary society.

This is not to diminish the enormous value of the faculty and professionals who trained you. We learn many valuable lessons in training. We often find mentors, advocates, and perhaps lifelong friends among the faculty. In addition, our shared production experiences with classmates can spark extraordinary moments of learning, collaboration, creativity, and discovery. And these classmates often become lifelong colleagues. Such relationships may prove important to your future. I have no doubt that you provided the artistic vision and leadership needed for the shows that you directed, but the situation was not comparable to the working world of professional theatre. While each of your classmates collaborated with you to achieve your directorial vision, all of you were learning on the job.

However, adopting the working methods that you used in training won't work in the professional theatre. Your practice in training often uses a highly collaborative and lengthy process. In the profession, you will need to lead the assembled creative team and company in a prescribed amount of time. In no way am I endorsing the opposite type of director—the controlling autocrat. By its nature, theatre is a deeply collaborative endeavor, especially when the artists with whom you work possess talent, experience, and lively imaginations. In fact, being inflexible and dictatorial in rehearsal is a surefire way to shut down professionals and destroy the potential of any show. However, you are responsible for the artistic vision required to create a thrilling show, and the leadership skills to elicit the best possible artistry and performance from everyone involved, no matter the many different levels of training, craft, talent, personality, and experience. For instance, the company may include a brilliant resident designer; a young, untrained actor; weary stage crew members; a deeply experienced but highly opinionated actor; a novice choreographer, and/or an overwhelmed but gifted craftsperson.

Directing for the subsidized or not-for-profit theatres

The typical missions of subsidized or not-for-profit theatre companies are devoted to artistic excellence in the creation of theatrical performances that entertain and serve the communities in which they are located. A few began in the early decades of the twentieth century, converting from amateur to professional theatres, including Birmingham Rep (UK) and Dallas Theatre Center (US). Rebelling against the financial models and commercial programming of the West End and Broadway, these theatres sought to produce seasons of classics, modern plays, and new works that were relevant, informative, and enriching. When Barry Jackson founded a new company in Birmingham in 1911, he stated, "The Rep's stated mission was 'to enlarge and increase the aesthetic sense of the public ... to give living authors an opportunity of seeing their works performed, and to learn something from the revival of the classics; in short to serve an art instead of making that art serve a commercial purpose.'"[16]

After the Second World War, many new regional or rep theatres were founded on both sides of the Atlantic. After introducing London audiences to the works of Samuel Beckett and Harold Pinter, Sir Peter Hall established the Royal Shakespeare Company in 1960 to realize his vision of a resident ensemble of actors, directors, and designers producing both modern and classic texts. Hall sought to re-establish William Shakespeare as the greatest playwright of all time, one whose plays demanded a distinctive style, and boldly imaginative productions. Because of their "subsidized" or "not-for-profit" designation, these theatres have a deeper sense of mission and purpose in serving the community and improving the world around them, through advancing the art and practice of theatre and making authentic connections with their audiences, artists, and community.

Between the 1950s and 1990s, the subsidized/not-for-profit fields in both countries grew substantially with remarkable support from governments and/or national foundations. Dozens of new theatre companies were established, and existing companies expanded their programming. All of it led to a frenzy of building new facilities in urban centers. As these theatres became institutionalized, they faced increased financial and business pressure to maintain and make additional income to support ever-increasing staffs and facilities; they did so by building audiences, adding additional programs, and renting their spaces. With the political and economic upheavals of the late 1980s and early 1990s, theatres faced new pressures. Subscription and single-ticket sales, corporate and foundation support, and government subsidy began a slow decline across several decades. As a sector, these theatres kept their commitment to work of substance and significance for their audiences, but they were also obliged to produce more broadly popular fare and undertake co-productions and even presenting to attract larger audiences, in order to pay the bills and keep the artistic product strong.

For many years, regional companies waited for the latest Broadway or West End hit to complete their season selection. New York and London were considered the primary creator and producer of new plays and musicals. Today that situation is reversed. Now it is the subsidized theatres who develop and originate the large majority of plays and musicals premiering in New York and London. Creating new work is now a major part of the mission for most not-for-profit theatres.

In the subsidized theatre, the director reports directly to the artistic director. At the larger regional theatres, there are often more human or financial resources than can be found at all but the largest theatres in New York or London. In many rep or regional theatres, the director may enjoy an artistic freedom and authority to create her personal artistic vision of the play not found in the commercial theatre. However, a freelance director will also be expected to work well with staff and company members. In addition, freelance directors may be asked to contribute in other areas, especially in fundraising and marketing activities.

Directing in the commercial theatre

The basic goal of the commercial theatre is straightforward—to make money. It is a for-profit enterprise. Producers are drawn to commercial theatre for many other reasons as well, including the love of musicals or plays, theatre people, the "magic of theatre," the glamour of Broadway or the West End, or to support the next generation of artists and shows. Of course, each hopes to produce the next great, successful musical that changes the art form and broadens the audience (e.g., *Hamilton*), but the bottom line is always front of mind.

Broadway musicals now cost anywhere from $8–$25 million. The time and effort required by a lead producer to raise the necessary money to produce a major musical on Broadway has increased significantly. The financial risk is very high, because only 20–25 percent of Broadway shows earn back their original investment. An even smaller portion of those musicals make a profit, and a very small sliver of those become mega-hits that create income for years to come (e.g., *Jersey Boys* or *Phantom of the Opera*). Although it is far cheaper to mount a Broadway play, at $3–$5 million, the odds of success are no better.

Therefore, you could argue that the commercial theatre is a form of gambling. That high level of financial risk gives the lead producer(s) and major investors enormous power over the director or director/choreographer. Although the director is hired by the lead producer, he or she can find themselves answering to many different masters. Budgeting, marketing, and even creative decisions are sometimes decided by committee (as the number of investors has grown exponentially). The director's task expands to successfully navigating extra layers of politics, dealing with large egos and handling the many backers who want to influence every aspect of the show not to mention the stars onstage. Today, Broadway and West End plays often succeed by hiring "star actors." In practice, one of the great challenges in directing commercially is identifying "who's the boss?" or "who really makes the decisions?" Is the boss the lead producer, the general manager, the star, the composer, or an entertainment corporation such as Disney Theatricals? For the director and/or choreographer, it's a thrilling, high octane, and complicated challenge. It brings great risk, but also great potential for artistic and financial success and widespread recognition.

Directing for conservatory or university programs

A professional director is often invited to direct acting students in academic or conservatory productions. Given the varying levels of talent, progress in training, experience, and skill level, directing young actors (often with remarkable talent and enthusiasm but little experience) requires a more structured approach than is often the case with professional actors. When a faculty member is not available to coach students in rehearsal, your duties may expand to include text/verse work, finding intentions and operative words, and unearthing character information from the script. You may need to lead each actor to build a structural foundation for her or his role in order to repeat key character and storytelling moments. The director may need to force the young actor not to settle for the first choice but keep pursuing better choices, or to help the actor map the arc of character. It's invigorating and demanding, but very rewarding work. If done well, the director can benefit greatly as student actors bring an enthusiasm, commitment, and gratitude to the work that is rarely found in the professional theatre. The danger of directing too frequently in conservatories is pedantry. This can lead to a condescending and "professorial" approach which will backfire when directing professional actors. Controlling every choice or assuming a lack of experience or expertise is unwise. Treating professionals like students is immediately perceived as condescending (it is!), and it often kills creative solutions from actors in rehearsal, who otherwise can help solve your staging or storytelling problems better than you alone. And shutting down a company often undermines the full realization of your concept and the creation of a unified and committed ensemble.

For the recent graduate, the different expectations and conditions of these sectors of the field underscores the need for continuous self-education. To work in multiple arenas, you need to learn the skills, techniques and tools, and practices of each sector.

Finding a mentor

As you add to your directing resumé and build your network, devote time to finding a mentor. The common definition of "mentor" is an influential, senior sponsor and supporter who becomes/is a wise and trusted counselor. You may have had a mentor on the faculty of your training program. Now you need to add additional mentors who have considerable experience and stature in professional directing, who can help you improve your directing, and who can advance your professional opportunities. Michael Langham taught me most of what I know about Shakespeare: table work, verse as action, character, structure, and staging, as well as the need for specific "actable" direction. Because he began working in theatre during his four-and-a-half years as a prisoner of war in Nazi Germany, Langham was driven, haunted, obsessive, brilliant, compelling, and often ruthless in his notes to actors. Mark Lamos (Artistic Director, Hartford Stage Company & Westport County Playhouse, with an extensive directing career in theatre and opera at Lincoln Center Theatre, Metropolitan Opera, Santa Fe Opera, Moscow Pushkin Theatre, The Stratford Festival, and more) pushed me to move beyond the traditional storytelling of active verse, plot, and character that Langham had taught me. Lamos freed my directorial imagination and taught me how to engage the artistry of my collaborators to create a bold new vision for each production. His advice was perceptive, cogent, and wise about directing and artistic direction. Having had Langham as his own directing mentor, Lamos brought full circle my conceptual work, my approach to directing, and my pursuit of artistic leadership.

Your search for a mentor must be intentional and proactive. Here are some suggested steps:

1   Create a list of directors whose work you most admire. Jot down why you are attracted to or impressed by their work. What does each bring to directing that is imaginative, new, sophisticated, astonishing, or invigorating? What captures your attention about her work? What specifically do you want to learn from this director?

2   Once you identify a director, push yourself to see every production she directs. Jot down your thoughts on each show. What did this director bring to the show? What conceptual, staging or storytelling devices worked best? When did the show succeed and when did it misfire? Why and why not?

3   Find out all the information you can on this director. Check online for interviews or writings, attend a lecture or post-show discussion by her, take a class or seminar she is teaching, and talk with colleagues, students, actors, designers, and more who have worked with her. Read the book she's written. Jot down thoughtful questions to ask when you meet.

4   Look for opportunities to meet and/or talk with her.

5   **Don't stalk!**

As you see more theatre, expand the list of directors you admire and hope to assist. In the meantime, take any assisting job you can. Although you may never have an opportunity to work with a specific director, by following these steps you are beginning to further refine your aesthetic and artistic vision. This proactive search for mentors is a far superior use of your time and energy than sending out dozens of cover letters and resumés to professionals who don't know you or your directing.

Finding collaborators and colleagues

Theatre is fundamentally a collaborative enterprise. You need to find and attract collaborators and colleagues even at this early stage in your career. Begin to build a circle of friends, actors, designers, playwrights, and perhaps donors who may help you create your shows now or later. Follow the same process that you used for mentors. Jot down notes, keep a database or add those you admire to your social media sites. And stay in touch.

This continuous pursuit of mentors and associates will inspire you, spark conversations and debates, arm you with insider's knowledge, and refine your artistic goals.

2

Understanding the Business of Theatre

As you continue to direct in a variety of situations, you should learn about the theatrical unions. In the United Kingdom, Equity[1] is the trade union that represents artists from across the entire spectrum of arts and entertainment. Equity's membership includes actors, singers, dancers, choreographers, stage managers, theatre directors and designers, variety and circus artists, standup comedians, television and radio presenters, walk-on and supporting artists, models, stunt performers and directors, and theatre fight directors. The Broadcasting, Entertainment, Cinematograph and Theatre Union (BECTU) represents theatre production and technical workers' and the Writers' Guild of Great Britain (WGGB) and the Musicians' Union (MU) cover writers and musicians, respectively. Equity negotiates multi-year "collective bargaining agreements" (CBAs) with organizations representing different sectors of the theatre field. For directors, Equity negotiates an array of CBAs that set minimum fees, benefits, terms, and working rules for many different categories, including major subsidized companies, subsidized and non-subsidized repertory companies, commercial theatre, fringe theatre, opera, drama schools, West End shows, and "No. 1" touring productions. Equity also has an area and committees for stage directors.[2] The union negotiates with two major "collective bargaining units": the Society of London Theatres[3]

(SOLT) for commercial shows in the West End and on No. 1 Tours, and UK Theatre[4] for all subsidized theatres and others.

In the United States, Stage Directors and Choreographers Society[5] (SDC) represents directors and choreographers. Its "mission is to foster a national community of professional stage Directors and Choreographers by protecting the rights, health, and livelihoods of all our Members; to facilitate the exchange of ideas, information, and opportunities, while educating the current and future generations about the role of Directors and Choreographers; and to provide effective administrative, negotiating, and contractual support." SDC covers directors and choreographers (and now fight directors) working in the following areas: Broadway and National tours, Off-Broadway, Association of Non-Profit Theatre Companies, New York City (ANTC), Resident Theatre/League of Resident Theatres (LORT), Resident Summer Stock Companies/Council of Resident Stock Theatres (CORST), Dinner Theatre/Dinner Theatre Agreement (DTA), Regional Musical Theatre (RMT), and Outdoor Musical Stock (OMS). SDC also provides Tier, Regional, Commercial, and Special contracts to protect Members who wish to work for organizations not covered by or referenced in one of the above CBAs.

CBAs are often more complicated in the US because there are many different unions which cover the field in addition to SDC. Other unions include: Actors Equity Association (AEA) for actors and stage managers; United Scenic Artists (USA) represents designers and certain craftspeople; The International Alliance of Theatrical Stage Employees (IATSE) has jurisdiction over stagehands, box office, and more; the Writers Guild of America (WGA) represents writers, and the American Federation of Musicians (AFM) has responsibility for musicians. When directing in major urban cities, several other unions can be involved. Some CBAs are negotiated on a national basis; others, like IATSE, on a local basis (between theatres and local union chapters).

To join Equity (UK) or SDC (US), you must provide evidence of one paid professional directing job that hired you on an SDC or Equity contract. That requirement appears to be a "Catch-22." How do you get a union job when you are not a member of the union? In practice, it may take some time, but the process is relatively straightforward. When any covered theatre or organization offers you a directing contract, you're qualified to join the union.

A more difficult question is deciding **when** to join the directors' union. If you live in Chicago or Manchester, there are many non-union theatre companies, and you can gain valuable directing experience at several theatres prior to joining the union. If you live in a community with only a couple of professional theatres on union agreements, it might be best to wait a few years. Remember, once you join either trade union, you cannot accept work without a union contract. Joining too early may deny you several opportunities. Next, there are the financial costs. In 2017, joining Equity as a theatre director required a one-off fee of £30 and an annual subscription ranging from £125 to £2,508, based upon your gross annual income from the profession. For SDC, there was an initiation fee of $2,000 and annual membership fee of $240, plus an annual assessment of 2.5 percent on all fees or royalties earned under SDC contracts.

Driven by the idea that "free market capitalism" would solve the economic and societal struggles of their countries, Prime Minister Margaret Thatcher and President Ronald Reagan, waged war on labor unions in the 1980s and weakened the unions' power and influence. This agenda has gathered steam with a series of conservative, business-friendly politicians. Today twenty-eight states in the US have "right to work" statutes that prohibit companies with collective bargaining agreements from compelling an employee to join a union or pay any costs for membership. In the UK, similar laws prevent a professional theatre from requiring you to join a union.

However, if you want to advance in the field, you will need to join the director's union at some point. Membership will protect and ensure your future fees, benefits, working conditions, and pension. In addition, unions supply considerable help and legal aid during any contractual dispute. They also provide many opportunities to learn and connect with other directors.

An agent or a manager

An agent works for a talent agency that is licensed by the state and franchised by the union. That gives the agent the legal right to solicit employment for clients, and then negotiate contracts on their behalf. Agents work on commission, which by law or industry practice is 10 percent of the negotiated salary or fee. Managers (sometimes called "personal managers") handle fewer clients and have a much wider role. They are responsible for their client's entire career path as well as for coordinating other members of the artist's "team" in the enhancement and promotion of the artist's career. Personal managers are not regulated either by state law or union regulations, and therefore have no legal, union or franchise restrictions imposed upon their commission structure. They cannot set up interviews, auditions or negotiate contracts, but are often actively involved in introducing directors to agents, producers, and higher levels of opportunity. Managers typically charge between 10 and 15 percent. Managers are much more useful for actors and directors in the television, cable, and film industry. Early and emerging career directors are better off pursuing an agent who represents theatre directors. The most effective way to find one is by asking your mentors, the directors you assist, or your colleagues. Although agencies may post whom they represent, the list is often limited to high-profile clients. Attracting and securing an agent will be discussed in an upcoming chapter.

Although it can be discouraging, you should be aware of the challenges facing every professional director. In a letter to the editor of *American Theatre*, SDC executive director Laura Penn wrote, "In 2016, 1,037 freelance SDC members worked exclusively in the non-profit theatre. On average they earned $14,695.04 (gross) through their work directing. In that same year, 89 members, or 9 percent, made $40,000 or more. There are exactly three freelance directors working in the non-profits who earned $100,000 last year. The success of the anonymous freelance director featured in the article, who earned $45,000, is not typical—although we deeply wish it were. Obviously most, if not all, freelance directors are also teaching, temping, or running Airbnbs out of their homes."[6]

According to a report[7] by the Stage Directors UK, a new advocacy organization for professional theatre and opera directors, a survey revealed that the median annual wage for a stage director in 2013–2014 was only £5,000. For subsidized theatres, fees ranged from £670 to just under £7,000 (apart from the National and the RSC).

At the same time, Penn believes (as I do) that we have arrived at a critical juncture for the professional theatre. If the past decade has focused on the new works and the primacy of playwrights and musical creative teams, might the next be focused on theatre directors? I think so. To stay relevant and appealing to twenty-first-century audiences, the theatre must reinvent itself with a new generation of leaders—namely, directors. This evolution demands fiercely determined, and visionary directors.

Staying alive

In this transition period between training and finding work, don't forget to live your life and keep your art alive. That means taking care of yourself physically and emotionally and nurturing your creativity and curiosity.

Explore whatever activities feed your imagination and spirit that are not related to the theatre. Go to museums or art galleries, create a social media persona or blog, watch all the films by a brilliant director, join social or political causes, volunteer at homeless shelters, attend fairs, festivals or events in other communities and cultures, attend church or research the major religions of the world, explore other creative endeavors, participate in sports, fitness or meditation, read books on psychology or psychiatry, and pursue any personal avocations that fascinate you. Get your passport and travel to other countries and visit other cultures. All of these activities will inform and enrich your directing in many unforeseen ways. And they will give you great life experiences.

Part II

Your First Professional Job

3

Interviewing for the Job

Congratulations! A professional theatre has contacted you about directing a show.

Typically, the artistic director or producer's assistant/representative will contact you, and ask about your "availability and interest" for a specific production. This contact is **not** an offer; the phrase "availability and interest" means: (1) are you free to direct this show on the scheduled dates? (i.e., first rehearsal through opening night), and (2) are you interested in directing this specific play or musical?

Check your availability against your other responsibilities (in work **and** life), but also factor in time for everything that needs to be accomplished before rehearsals begin. You will need to complete an in-depth script analysis, develop your concept and point-of-view, and determine the artistic and production needs of the show. You will also spend time meeting and working with the creative team (e.g., designers, coaches, dramaturg, etc.), and the artistic and production staffs of the theatre. Unless the show is pre-cast, you also need to include time (typically set by the theatre) for casting, including auditions, callbacks, and offers. If you're directing a musical, double the audition time to include singing and dancing calls. If you are already committed to a project for a theatre, conservatory, or arts organization, this is a moral gut check moment. How will the other organization be affected if you renege on your prior commitment? Will it create a burden on the theatre or damage the project? Burning bridges in the theatre is a dangerous habit, because the same people or organizations you anger or hurt often reappear throughout your career. Following my first season assistant directing at The Stratford Festival in Canada, Artistic Director John Hirsch offered me another assisting job with additional responsibility and money. Late in the pre-production process, a guest director had given Hirsch an extensive list of conflicts and absences. Hirsch wanted me to cover multiple rehearsals and indicated that he hoped to establish an extended relationship between the theatre and myself. I was frustrated at being offered yet another job assisting. Also, my earlier experience was difficult as I confronted the challenges of "directing" substantial portions of a show for an absentee director without the proper authority to do so. I quickly said no, and Hirsch was disappointed and angry. In fact, my decision hurt my relationship with Hirsch and The Stratford Festival as well as my chances to work at larger theatres.

Gauging your "interest" can be more challenging. As an early career director, you need the job, the directing credit, and—definitely—the money. Moreover, you can start a relationship with this theatre and its artistic director. If offered, you will eagerly accept the job. However, it's wise to take a breath and review the play or musical that you're being asked to direct. Regardless of your level of familiarity with the piece, follow these steps, prior to the interview.

1 **Experience the play/musical.** Read the script or book/lyrics and listen to the score in one, undistracted sitting. Although I strongly recommend that you keep a personal journal or notebook to jot down thoughts and ideas (as well as for every script you read or production you see), **don't take notes the first time through**. As best you can, read and listen as if it's a new musical. In other words, try to perceive the piece as if you were an audience member who has never seen it or read it. When you finish, reflect on your immediate, visceral reactions. Write down your "first" impressions, emotional responses, observations, and thoughts. In my professional experience, one's first reactions to a script are frequently the most useful. For me, the immediacy and impact of the first reading holds vital pointers to the production I hope to create for the actors and the audiences.

    I do **not** recommend watching a current production of the show at this stage. It's too easy to adopt or reject specific solutions or ideas. Only when you have completed a thorough analysis should you buy a ticket and see it in performance—and then only when you are having difficulty visualizing the show onstage. Also, avoid watching films of it.

Film versions of plays and musicals are often revised, heavily cut, and re-arranged (or all three). Tim Burton's *Sweeney Todd* cut two songs, "Kiss Me" and "Ladies in Their Sensitivities," re-orchestrated the score, reordered scenes and reassigned lines to support his dark, horrifying, and surreal concept of Sondheim's classic. Baz Luhrmann's thrilling, violent, visually stunning, and captivating *Romeo and Juliet* cut about 40 percent of Shakespeare's original text, changed the order of scenes and speeches, and reassigned lines. Further, neither you nor the theatre can match the visual designs, the camera angles, special effects or production/design budgets of a movie. Don't be tempted.

2 **Read the play/musical again.** And consider the following questions: When did it "engage" you fully? (i.e., when did you "suspend your disbelief"?). What moments were astonishing, stimulating, and/or emotionally engaging? If you have read, seen, or worked on the play/ musical previously, what did you discover anew? What changed from your last experience of it? Your responses here are the **beginning** steps in shaping your directorial approach to the project. Resist jumping to staging ideas, and the temptation to immediately decide on your "concept."

Presuming that you are excited and inspired, or simply fascinated and intrigued by the piece, call the theatre and let them know that you are available and interested. If you can find absolutely no interest or merit in the script, talk with a friend or colleague, preferably someone who disagrees with your judgment. She may provide a different perspective. If you truly cannot admire anything in the script, consider your options. Don't accept a job if you despise the material. Cynicism and condescension towards a show can become toxic and spread quickly throughout a company. Your job is to find merit in the script and create solutions for production. If you don't believe in it, don't direct it. That's a rare occurrence in any directing career. If you think you must accept the job anyway, surround yourself with friends and colleagues who love the show and who can give you regular doses of insight and inspiration.

After you call the theatre, take another breath, because theatres often check the interest and availability of several directors at the same time.

Script, design, and production analysis

When and if the theatre sets up an interview, return to the script (and score). *Read the play and listen to the musical again.* This time, jot down notes, questions, ideas, and images as you read. Analyse the dramatic structure. Note the scenes and moments that are pivotal to the dramatic arc. What actions or events present the biggest challenges in staging and storytelling? Make a list of major artistic and production concerns and questions. These can include specific needs in casting, special effects, costumes, scenery, lighting, sound, music, etc. Quickly **make three lists** but keep them short and simple.

1 List the moments, scenes, and major events that you find most exciting, compelling, and fascinating? What fires your imagination and stirs your interest in it **as a director**?

2 List the moments, scenes and major events that are most important to **the dramatic storytelling**. Look at the plot, how the tension ebbs and flows, the surprises or revelations, and the conflicts leading to climax and resolution. Ask which are vital or pivotal to an audience's understanding of the story?

3 List the moments, scenes, and major events that are most challenging in **staging, design, and production**. For example, in Shakespeare's *The Tempest*, there are many scenes and moments that need clever staging and design, including the opening storm, the magical spells cast by Prospero and Ariel, the Harpy and the hellhounds terrifying and chasing the shipwrecked nobles, the disappearing banquet table, Prospero's pageant of Greek goddesses for Miranda and Ferdinand, and Prospero breaking his magical staff.

Compare and contrast the three lists. Are there any items on one list that don't appear on the other two? If the three lists don't align, figure out why. This exercise is very helpful in increasing your specific knowledge of the text, clarifying the most critical staging challenges, and most importantly, identifying conflicts between your emerging directorial concept and the storytelling needs of the script. This process helps you to avoid a common trap for directors which I call "Premature Concept Lock." This occurs when a director jumps to a dazzling or seductive concept without thoroughly knowing the play/text. When I've done this in the past, I've often painfully discovered in rehearsal that my concept doesn't work for a major scene. As a result, I've wasted valuable time and resources trying to achieve my concept.

Fortunately, most artistic directors have a well-developed nose for vaguely defined or questionable concepts. For instance, a director once pitched a concept to me for *Hamlet* that used the style of Film Noir-inspired graphic novels, because the show was being produced with young adult actors and for young audiences. As artistic director, I was very excited and intrigued by the idea, but I asked the director to explain how this concept would enhance or enrich the play in performance? Why is it relevant and exciting now? What does the concept require in staging, casting, design, and production to achieve? How does the concept support the action of important scenes, such as the appearances of the Ghost of Hamlet's Father, the play-within-the-play, and the duel between Hamlet and Laertes. In other words, how well does the concept work throughout the play? What does it add and what does it diminish in the play? Only after hearing his answers could I evaluate the concept and decide whether to hire him or not. I did.

Who are you working for?

If time permits, research the person with whom you're meeting and her theatre. If you don't know the artistic director or producer, talk with the people who have worked for her. Check online interviews, reviews, and production photos on the theatre's website or in the press. You're researching the leader's artistic vision and tastes, professional loves or hates, points-of-view, style of working, and achievements. If you've not seen a performance at the theatre, scan the theatre's website for its mission, vision, production history, and programming. Does the theatre's mission state what genre or type of theatre it produces (e.g., classics, new plays, plays by women, political theatre, theatre in non-traditional spaces, or community-created shows)? Does the website indicate specific preferences in aesthetics, style, practice, or point of view? Is Shakespeare produced "only in Renaissance costumes, sets, props, etc." or must it focus on "the acting and the text" with minimal design elements? Must every show reflect the diversity of the world today? Is the theatre devoted to hyper-realism . . . or fantastical spectacle?

Next, evaluate the ability of the theatre to support your vision for the production. The quickest way to do this is by looking up production photos of past and current shows online. These reveal the theatre's production values. Read the bios of artists and staff. What is the proportion of union vs non-union actors? Does the theatre use a resident company or hire local and/or out-of-town actors? Who regularly designs for the theatre? Contact Equity or SDC to find which agreement the theatre uses for the performance space in which you will direct. This research is done so that you can formulate your artistic vision based upon a realistic understanding of the theatre's resources.

The interview

During the interview, you will usually be asked why you want to direct this play, what excites you about it, and what directorial approach you have in mind. Express your excitement and interest for the show and this theatre. Give a dynamic description of your concept using examples from major moments or scenes throughout the script. Talk about what characters or ideas you want to focus on. Describe the experience you want to create for the actors, the artists, and the audience. Artistic directors want to hear your ideas and vision for the play, including your ideas about production and design, but they also want to get to know you as a person, an artist, and a director. Many of the best artistic director/freelance director interviews in my career covered an unexpectedly wide range of ideas, stories, and observations, not all of which related to the production.

These interviews can be as varied as the many personalities of artistic leaders. With luck, your conversation will be lively and friendly, and the artistic director will be responsive and excited about your vision and will enjoy the give-and-take of your conversation along with your insights and ideas. But don't count on it. The artistic director may be interviewing several directors, be distracted by the pressing problems of the day, or not know exactly what she wants. If the artistic director seems to outwardly show alarm or disapproval at some of your ideas, keep going and note it later in your journal. It may be disapproval or simply the way she responds to new ideas.

The latter part of the interview is a valuable time to gather as much information as you can, provided your interviewer is willing and has the time. Your questions should include:

- Why did she pick this play? For her theatre? At this time?
- Are there artistic principles or practices that the theatre adopts in terms of design, production scale and style, budget, etc.?
- How are creative teams selected? How much input will you have on designers, etc.? Are there resident designers? Have designers already been hired?
- How does casting work? Have any actors or artists been hired? Will the show be cast locally or out-of-town (e.g., New York, Seattle, London, Chicago, Glasgow, Los Angeles, Dublin, etc.)?
- What is the rehearsal and production schedule? Generally, how much time is spent in rehearsal hall, onstage and tech/dress rehearsals, and how many previews are scheduled before opening?

- Does the theatre hire coaches and designers beyond the usual (e.g., scenery, costumes, sound and lighting)? Will your show have composers for incidental music, speech and dialect coaches, or dramaturgs? For a musical, ask about the plan for music direction and choreography? Will the score be played live or pre-recorded? If live, what will be the orchestra's size?
- What's her timeline for a decision on hiring a director?

Unless you are offered the show on the spot, thank her for the opportunity to meet and talk about the show. Make notes of your interview in your journal and send a "thank you" note or email as soon as possible; don't gush, flatter or repeat your major ideas, but keep it simple and direct. Then put the possibility aside. That's very tough to do, but now your job is to wait until a decision is made. Unfortunately, it's common for some theatres or producers not to inform you if you didn't get the job. If you are rejected, **don't take it personally**, but start making another list—what you would do differently if you were an artistic director.

Directing Someone Else's Concept

Occasionally, an artistic director will tell you the concept that he wants for a particular play. This can be based on his artistic philosophy or taste, his experience with his audiences, the function the show serves in that season, or the theatre's past history of producing similar shows. For instance, an artistic director may request a "traditionally" staged production of *Romeo and Juliet*, that explores two themes: the star-crossed beauty of young love, and the hate-filled violence of the streets.

If this concept is sprung upon you in the interview, let the artistic director know of your surprise, but give it a shot anyway. Your extensive familiarity with the script gives you a significant advantage. Ask the artistic director to tell you more about his reasoning, and why he chose this vision. Brainstorm ideas for major moments in the show. Ask him more questions: What does he mean by "traditionally designed"? Does he mean late medieval or Renaissance, or any non-modern historical period? For both costumes and scenery? Ask him to elaborate upon his ideas about hate-filled violence and young love in the context of the play. Talk about the street brawls, sword fights, the death of Paris, and the two suicides. If you perceive a growing appreciation for your ideas, briefly describe your original concept but be ready to move on. If you need more time to consider his concept, ask if you can follow up with an email or a phone call.

If you decide to take the job and the pre-determined concept, make it your own. Embrace the overall ideas but put your own spin on its execution. Never pretend to embrace a pre-determined concept and then try to design and direct your production towards your original concept. Although the concept is not what you would have chosen, this is a terrific opportunity to grow by directing outside your comfort zone.

Negotiations and arrangements

If you are offered the job, negotiations with the business side of the organization will begin, usually with a managing director or a general/business manager. If you have an agent, she will take the offer and negotiate your contract. If not, you will need to negotiate for yourself. Check the SDC or Equity website and review the terms of the specific contract used by the theatre. If it's your first union job, this process is straightforward. You will be offered the minimum fee, associated benefits, etc. However, before you sign the contract, read any addenda or riders that have been attached, in case there are specific additional duties, policies, etc., that you must follow. Sign the contract in a timely manner and return it.

We've already reviewed the unions that cover directors and choreographers in each country. For the professional director, it's useful to learn the relevant work rules for your contract category, but also valuable to learn the relevant rules for other artists in the show. Focus on the rules that directly affect your job, especially those concerning casting, allowable lengths of rehearsals, required breaks and rest periods between calls, costume fittings, and safety and working conditions. Talk to the production manager about the work rules and practices pertaining to production personnel (e.g., craftspeople, stage crews, technicians, etc.) and guest artists (e.g., designers, voice and speech specialists, fight directors, conductors, musicians, etc.). Talk to your stage manager, who is the most valuable source of information regarding work rules and practices for actors and stage management staff.

4

The Director's Work in Pre-Production

As mentioned in the first chapter, the pre-production period often continues for months before the first rehearsal and includes multiple tasks and deadlines, including:

- in-depth script work, research, and preparation;
- refining or reinventing your artistic vision or concept;
- meetings with designers and production staff, submission of preliminary designs, approvals, and final designs;
- casting and hiring.

These tasks frequently overlap, and occasionally will happen simultaneously. This can present a serious challenge for any freelance director. The schedule depends on several factors, including how far in advance of rehearsals you are hired; the available time and resources of the theatre's staff who are busy producing other shows for the current season; and the level of effective planning and communication among different departments (i.e., artistic, literary, casting, production, and management) at the theatre. Many small to mid-size theatres do not have separate departments and each staff member assumes multiple duties. When you find yourself directing in such situations, you must take the responsibility to "self-produce" and figure out how to fill the most important gaps in the pre-production process.

If you did not receive a detailed information packet with your contract, you should contact the production manager immediately for information. You will need a detailed rehearsal and performance schedule, a production/design schedule with dates for the Director/Designer Conference, and deadlines for the submission of preliminary designs, your review of the designs, requests for revisions, approvals by the theatre, and the submission of final designs. These dates will be staggered, because of the differently timed work flow of each member of the creative team. For instance, sound, lighting, and projection designers often cannot complete their designs until the scenic designer has finalized her production design. Make sure to ask the artistic and production staff about the theatre's expectations of a director at the director/designer conference. To save money, a theatre may hold a design conference on the telephone or by Skype or Facetime and communicate thereafter by email. If the theatre doesn't hold a director/designer conference, you should arrange one yourself, in whatever way you can afford. Typically, the theatre will expect you to present an exciting and inspiring artistic vision of the production at the conference. Many theatres also expect to see preliminary sketches, designs, visual research, and even staging ideas at this conference.

Next, you should contact the staff member responsible for casting. Request all pertinent information about the theatre's casting practices. Ask how casting works at this theatre: Is there a resident company? Is casting handled in-house or managed by an external casting director? Does the theatre "pre-cast" actors (by direct offer) prior to auditions? If the artistic director told you earlier that certain roles have been cast, confirm that information. And, most important, verify the planned size of the cast. Don't forget to ask about the casting schedule: what are the dates? Are there auditions at the theatre as well as in New York or Chicago or Los Angeles? This information will be invaluable to you in laying out and planning for the many tasks ahead.

Verify and verify again with the production manager that you have the correct script for the production. Surprisingly, mistakes or miscommunications regarding the official script can happen at several levels; discovering that you and the actors are using the wrong script during rehearsals is incredibly frustrating; and an enormous amount of precious time and energy will have been wasted! During season selection, artistic, literary, and production staffs may have worked with a specific printed edition or an early draft of the play. It is quite possible that you, the designers, and the production staff may be working from different scripts. The mistake can also easily occur at the industry level. The licensing agreement should stipulate the correct version of the play to be used, but that may not be correct. Ayad Akhtar's play, *Disgraced*, premiered at the America Theatre Company in Chicago in early 2012, and made its Off-Broadway debut at the Lincoln Center that year. In 2014, it premiered at The Bush Theatre in London and on Broadway. Widely produced in the US, *Disgraced* has also been produced in many European cities. Akhtar has rewritten the play frequently given the rising hatred and discrimination against Arab Americans. When producing it at the Denver Center in 2017, we discovered to our horror that we were not using the most current and correct version in rehearsals. We were using the one sent by his agent, but we had not verified and double checked the script with the playwright. Also, the sole rights to produce the play or musical may be controlled by an agent, a licensing house, or a producer, but these arrangements can change frequently. A producer may have bought the countrywide or worldwide rights to produce the show commercially. Some refuse to allow any other professional production before their planned or "hoped for" production in the West End or on Broadway. They might hold a series of workshops or investor readings to gauge interest, then hold on to the rights, let them go or begin licensing to other theatres. Other producers are more flexible, but only in select markets. For example, if Bette Midler wants to star in *Hello, Dolly!* on Broadway, the lead producer may refuse to grant rights elsewhere in the US, given her international star power combined with the reality that tourists now buy a large portion of tickets to any Broadway musical. Or the playwright's agent may be withholding performance rights for his client, in hopes of landing a film deal, a commercial production, or multiple productions at major resident theatres around the country. That said, nine out of ten plays and musicals that have been produced professionally several times are handled by a licensing house or publishing company. These companies often print the "official acting edition" to be used in all future productions. They include Samuel French, Music Theatre International, Methuen, TCG, Dramatists Play Services, Rodgers & Hammerstein, and others.

Ask for any restrictions or approvals listed in the licensing agreement, which may include approval of the director or cast by the author or his heirs.

The theatre normally undertakes this task, but if there is no literary department, it's wise for a director to inquire with the managing director, who negotiated and signed the agreement. Recently, the executor of Edward Albee's estate caused a public outcry when he pulled the rights of a production of *Who's Afraid of Virginia Woolf?* that featured an all-Black cast. The licensing rights for *West Side Story* include the directive that the original Broadway choreography of Jerome Robbins must be used and credited in any professional production.

If you are directing a world premiere or recently premiered new play, check with both the theatre and the playwright. Confirm you have the latest draft and find out if the playwright intends to write a new draft or make significant revisions before rehearsals begin. Later in the book, "Directing New Plays and Musicals" will provide information and advice for directing new plays or musicals in workshops and in productions.

Immersion in the script

The biggest mistake directors make is not knowing the script well enough before settling on their concept, approving designs, casting, or beginning rehearsals. This is **the** opportunity to immerse yourself in the script. It is not to be wasted.

Read the script or review the book/lyrics and score again.

And again.

And again.

And again.

You get the point. There is no better method to prepare yourself for directing a show than repeated reading and reviewing. A British colleague and friend, Gavin Cameron-Webb, has directed many classics, including several Shakespeare plays. His pre-rehearsal process has included typing the entire play on his laptop, whether it's *Romeo and Juliet* or *Cymbeline*. His purpose is two-fold: to develop a deep and intimate knowledge of the play, word by word, line by line, and scene by scene; and to create a script that can be easily cut, revised, reordered, and reprinted. Although you can now download a text version of any Shakespeare play, its accuracy, spelling, and punctuation is unpredictable, and a simple download does not give you a deeper understanding of the text.

Next, consult your observations about the script and return to your earlier notes from the interview. For a large-scale or complicated musical or play, I advise turning these notes into more formal documents. This practice can be especially useful for many new plays and musicals, which have adopted the structure of a screenplay, using many scenes and multiple locations with fast transitions, and special visual effects. Create three documents. The first document I prepare is a **Scene/Character Breakdown.** This spreadsheet includes each actor line, the role(s) each plays, scene number, page number, and page count (for Shakespeare plays, I also add total line count). Remember to include "townspeople," "lords and ladies," "the chorus of drag queens," or "a mob carrying torches," as well as any playwright-prescribed doubling. Give each scene a "nickname" that states the essence of the scene. For a musical, the nickname is often the title of the song in that portion of a scene. For example, it can be "Angel Crashes through Ceiling" in Tony Kushner's *Angels in America, Part One.*

Next create a **Plot/Scene Breakdown.** Include the earlier nicknames for scenes, scene and page numbers, etc., but focus on bullet points of action (i.e., what happens in the scene), and make notes on location, time, special effects, and problems to be solved (e.g., Faust descends into Hell, or the rushing stream into which naked men jump in Frank Galati's adaptation of *The Grapes of Wrath*).

Last, create a **Character Descriptions** document. For each character, list age range, gender, physical characteristics, relationships to other roles, ethnicity or cultural background (if it's relevant to your production or the play, such as *Fences* by August Wilson), plus any specific information provided by the playwright. I also include special needs (e.g., foreign language or dialect needs, dance, stage combat expertise, singing ability, etc.) and any unique skills (such as playing sitar, experience in puppetry, clogging, unicycling, etc.). This document not only helps me write the "Casting Breakdowns" for auditions, but also prevents me from casting an actor who cannot fulfill the necessary requirements of the role. No matter how brilliantly an actor reads for D'Artagnan in *The Three Musketeers,* if he doesn't have the training and stamina to effectively fight with swords and daggers six or seven times each performance, eight times a week, don't cast him. For musicals, consult with the music director and choreographer and ask about how to add singing ranges and dance requirements for each character. Finally, I note any roles that I want to cast with non-traditional, diverse, gender neutral, differently abled, or other unconventional performers.

For a classical play or any script no longer in copyright, ask the artistic or literary staff if there are any "house rules" regarding the cutting of roles, scenes or speeches, emendations of words and lines, or rearrangement of scenes. One prominent regional theatre recently told me that no production can exceed two-and-a-half hours including intermission—that could be a very tough challenge if you're directing *King Lear* or *Hamlet*. Deciding on cuts and script changes prior to the director/design conference and casting is immensely valuable. It saves an enormous amount of time and energy. Cuts also change design needs.

Admittedly, completing this amount of paperwork is a judgment call. When you're directing a small cast, one-set show, you may not need this level of detail and information. If you are blessed with an assistant director or intern from the theatre's staff, parts of these tasks can be delegated. Stage managers often create their own version of a scene/character breakdown to help them track the show, make accurate rehearsal calls and fitting times, and plan transitions. However, you should be aware that freelance stage managers often start their contract only one week before rehearsals begin.

Your artistic vision

Now is the time to develop your concept for the show. Creating an inspiring, innovative, effective, and engaging directorial vision requires both an objective and a subjective approach to the play. In other words, you need to use both sides of your brain. After two centuries of research into brain function, we now know that the left hemisphere guides your logical, sequential, analytical, and objective decisions; and the right hemisphere guides your creative, intuitive, holistic, and subjective impulses. To keep the flame of your passion, ideas, and interests burning, brainstorm ideas, follow impulses and intuitions, imagine visual images, and explore personal feelings. Express strong opinions and reactions. During this time, the pragmatic should never interfere with the creative and artistic. Finding time for reflection and daydreaming is extremely difficult in today's hyper-connected world, I know, but you must discover your own way of seeking creative stimuli as an artist. Experiment and find the activities that help you explore and test ideas. Is it talking with colleagues or friends? Or writing down freeform musings? Do creative ideas emerge when you're walking your dog, visiting a zoo, listening to music, playing tennis or golf, or seeing a performance art installation? Are you inspired by similar works of art: paintings, novels, musicals, museum exhibits, or films?

As you let your right brain find creative ideas, bring analytical research into play using your left brain. Examine the script's source material and read other works by the same playwright. Research the historical, political, social, and cultural issues in the play; learn about the ideas, fashions, architecture, art, norms of public and private behavior, including acts that were considered transgressive or controversial at the time. Investigate the theatrical practices that were employed when the play was written. For me, a "period play" is anything written or set more than 25 years in the past. The available resources on the internet allow access to interviews with many creative teams and playwrights. For instance, you can find Lynn Nottage discussing *Ruined* or Mike Bartlett talking about *King Charles III*. Both plays offer rich opportunities for research into the cultures and time periods they cover. This period of research and thought can be an especially informative and stimulating time for a director.

However, research can become irrelevant and destructive when it leads to an obsessive quest to discover a classical playwright's "original intention" or to pedantically re-create an historical period. To avoid this, I use a litmus test to compare my "findings" against the expectations of the theatre, its artists, and its audiences. For example, if the theatre and its audiences are steeped in "Original Practice" productions of Shakespeare's plays, that use Elizabethan costumes and "all-male" casts, your innovative, irreverent, contemporary, and gender-neutral production of the script may fall flat or worse. While a traditional production may reinforce the audience's conviction that this is the "correct way to produce Shakespeare," setting it in later periods, such as the frequently chosen mid-nineteenth to mid-twentieth century, may surprise and thrill the same audiences, because these periods can more easily illuminate class and power differences, politics and privilege, character behaviors, social rules of courtship, love and marriage, etc.

Your analytical research will define "what the play is fundamentally about." Some refer to this as the "theme," but I believe that is too reductive, because your own idiosyncratic point-of-view must be included. Your concept must include your strong opinion, attitude, conviction, and passion about the play, as well at the experience you want to create for artists and audiences. Otherwise, your production will result in a clear and well-staged production that lacks spice, relevance, and creative fire. As your right brain helps you discover your vision, your left brain helps you articulate that vision. Try to avoid a highly academic or profoundly intellectual concept unless the play absolutely demands it. Write an informal conceptual statement which combines your emerging artistic ideas with your practical analysis of the play's staging, design, and production. Revisit this statement often, revise it, and elaborate on it. This process of refining your concept while considering the pragmatic ways to fulfill your vision will be invaluable as you work through the design and production elements of the show.

As you prepare for the director/designer conference, review your notes on any production you saw at the theatre that hired you. If you haven't seen a production in the theatre space in which you will be directing, ask to view archival videos or video footage shot for commercials or interviews. Both may be restricted by union agreements, but ask for access. Check online for production photos of past productions of similar scale and size. Evaluate the resources and capacity in design by observing the production values the theatre consistently achieves. Prepare for the upcoming conference by reviewing your notes on the importance of each design element for the script and your concept. Be specific. Prioritizing the design needs will inform your choice of designers. When asked to direct an upcoming regional/rep production of *The Curious Incident of the Dog in the Night-Time*, I reviewed the script and my notes several times before deciding which design elements were most important to my artistic vision of the script. Did I want to incorporate similar technological, scenic, projection, and sound designs as were created for the original production at the Royal National Theatre and subsequent commercial runs in the West End and on Broadway? Naturally, I did not. Although the stage directors' work is not protected by copyright laws, the work of the designers is. However, copying **exactly** the overall production design and direction is considered violation of intellectual property in the US. The laws are complicated, but some union agreements now include copyright protections for the director in Broadway productions. There are no relevant copyright laws for stage directors in the UK, but protections exist to prevent replicating a production's direction and design.

Having personally toured the set for *The Curious Incident* on Broadway, I realized that the specific not-for-profit theatre for which I was directing could never afford the tremendous cost of the many high-definition projectors and computers that were used in the original production, much less the additional design fees. What fascinated me about directing the play was inventing a different directorial, design, and style of performance in staging this mystery novel turned play. What new and innovative ideas could we use to establish the chaotic and disruptive world of the story as experienced by its leading character, a 15-year-old boy with Asperger's syndrome? We had the wonderful challenge of finding new ways to tell and to illuminate Christopher's courageous, harrowing, and remarkable journey to find his mother in London.

The creative team

The next part of the process is working with the theatre to assemble a **Creative Team** which will include all the designers, and possibly a music director, choreographer, and at larger theatres, various coaches and specialists, etc. This process is both a discussion and a negotiation between you and the artistic director and/or production manager. If this is your first professional directing gig for a theatre, or the first time working at a theatre with a much higher level of resources, some decisions may have been made for you. For example, many subsidized theatre companies now use "resident" staff designers or a small set of frequently hired designers. Others hire design teams for each theatre space across the entire season. Others hire a combination of local and out-of-town designers. And, it should be said, some theatres will assign you designers without discussion. If you don't know their work, look online for websites, resumés, and bios.

Unless the creative team is already set, now is your opportunity to ask for the designers whom you want. You may include designers with whom you have worked, know well or admire. Pull out your notes on the shows you have seen and review your lists of designers of interest. This reinforces the need to keep notes of productions you have seen and an ongoing list of admired designers. It is equally important to frequently update your contacts and network, including the work of friends and classmates who have become working professional designers. Evaluate the level of experience, artistry, and accomplishment of any designer of interest. Does her work match or exceed the level of the theatre's current design and production levels? If not, reconsider. In negotiations and conversations with the theatre, recognize the value of a designer who regularly works at the theatre. She will have existing, positive relationships with the organization and its shops. She will also know how the theatre operates and how to achieve the best possible outcome.

Balance your desire to work with a highly esteemed or prominent designer with a measure of reality. Will the designer have a genuine interest in working with you, given your current resume and experience? With the theatre, given its resources? If you have a strong personal or professional relationship, he may say "yes." However, keep in mind that prominent designers expect and deserve higher fees and financial resources, including larger production budgets, extra travel, and often the addition of an assistant or associate designer. Successful designers are often juggling multiple projects, which may significantly reduce the time they can devote to you and your show. You may end up working more with their associate or assistant during tech, dress rehearsals, and previews.

Several months earlier the production staff will have created schedules for the entire season, from design/director conferences through to rehearsal and performances for all the shows. They use this information to create budgets for each production based upon the script and the human and financial resources available, as determined by the producer or managing director (who will have projected earned and subsidized income and expenses in every department). Hopefully, there has been information sharing between artistic, production, and management leaders, and the artistic director will have given specific information regarding the design, casting, and other producing needs, and the role that he hopes each show will fulfill within the entire season. Many of these decisions regarding schedules, resources, and budgets will have been made many months in advance. In addition, the current season priorities (e.g., getting the shows up, selling them, raising money) can collide with the next season's priorities (e.g., selecting shows, scheduling, budgeting, hiring directors, and designers). As a freelance director, it's important to find out what assumptions have been made and what resources have been allocated for your show. Verify the show's budget and ask for any additional needs you anticipate as soon as possible.

Timely communication with the theatre regarding assembling the creative team is vital, because both you and the production manager are trying to engage the best design team as soon as possible, to ensure they are hired before their schedules fill up. Communicate with your designers as soon as they are hired. Send them a written version of your concept and approach to the play, with any thoughts on period, style, theatrical storytelling, and point-of-view. Include your cuts, changes and doubling of actors, and any images or relevant research you have done. Send them the three documents you prepared, namely your Scene/Character Breakdown, Plot/Scene Breakdown, and Character Descriptions. The first conversation is best held with the entire team in the same room, but logistics often mean Skype, Facetime, or phone conferencing. Articulate your artistic vision and engage their considerable talents and experience to help you and the theatre achieve it. Lead the conversation but encourage discussion and debate. I ask designers to challenge or question my conceptual approach and to offer alternative ideas. I like to ask the designers the same questions that I have asked myself: Why do they want to design this play **now**? What draws them to this play? What's most exciting or inspiring? What's most challenging? I also ask if any designer has designed this play or musical before and confess if I have directed it. This forces each of us to question the temptation to repeat a past production concept or design. One of the dangers of repeating your prior, successful production is that you often stifle new and better ideas; having brilliantly "solved" one production, you may cling to those old choices in design, acting, and storytelling that were so successful, despite having a new company of artists and staff, not to mention new audiences. This can diminish the excitement of production and lead to a dull performance. Later we will discuss the benefits of creating a signature production.

Director/designer conference

The director/design conference gives you an excellent opportunity to share with the artistic and production staff of the theatre the creative work that you and the designers have accomplished. Show them the most interesting and relevant visuals from your work, inspire and engage them and invite them on the journey to create the show you envision.

The Elevator Speech

As the director/designer conference approaches, I create an "elevator speech" about my concept. This practice is borrowed from the business world; it is an informal, pithy speech that's so short it can be delivered during an elevator ride. This is not the "blurb" that marketing departments write to sell the show. Rather, it is a 2–4 sentence "talk" which expresses my reason for, and passion in directing, this production. It will touch on my concept, how the show will be staged, and what will prove most exciting about the production. It's a cogent, articulate, passionate, and inspiring speech about my directorial vision for the musical or play. This elevator speech helps me inspire the theatre's staff, my creative team, and eventually the actors. I find it to be extremely useful because it forces me to decide what's most important and exciting to me about the upcoming production.

The schedule for the Director/Designer Conference typically begins with a group meeting with the artistic director, the production manager, all designers, any coaches or specialists, and production department heads. After introductions, you will be asked to present your concept for the production, then the designers will share their initial work. The day will include a visit to the theatre with designers, and a series of meetings, during which you will talk through the entire script with designers and relevant staff, either in group or individual settings. The larger group often reconvenes at the end of the day to review progress and confirm key dates.

Bring your own research, images, and visuals that you have been exploring to the conference. Ask the designers to share their work, including sketches, images from magazines and books, architectural photos or sketches, period or contemporary clothing fashions, quick drafts of ground plans, or anything inspiring or relevant to the show. Review and explore the materials they provide and explain your initial choices. When directing *Measure for Measure*, I shared images of paintings by Gustav Klimt and his protégé Egon Schiele, because their work openly explored the sexual, erotic, and romantic relationships of early twentieth-century Vienna (as part of the Secession). I was drawn to Klimt's erotic paintings of beautiful and sensual lovers trapped in golden layers of circles, tiles, and ornamentation. By contrast, Schiele's used pallid skin tones with tinges of green, purple, and orange to depict his lovers, prostitutes, and their clients. Combined with the twisted bodies and the garish colors of the clothing, makeup or hair, Schiele's work implied a feverish, sickly, and disturbing sexuality. To me, these two artists represented the grandeur and decadence of Shakespeare's Vienna, with its extremes of power, class, corruption, religious belief, romance and lust, sexism and sexual squalor. At the conference, the set and costume designer brought a remarkable book by Japanese photographer Kunihiro Takuma. *Rebirth* features close-up photographs of multiple layers of paint, rust, and decay from manmade and natural objects. This book became vitally important to my concept of the show, because it supplied the principal metaphor for my concept of the play's setting. At first glance, the Viennese court appeared to possess great beauty, wealth and power, but it's soon revealed as corrupt, hypocritical, and weak because it took advantage of the poverty, sexual squalor, violence, and oppression of the people in its streets. Although the art of Schiele and Klimt appeared in the scenic and costume designs, my "North Star" became the photographs of Takuma.

The first meeting at the conference will include the artistic director or his appointed staff member. If he questions your concept and the design work, try to avoid becoming defensive; instead discuss your objectives and reasoning. If that doesn't work, ask to meet privately with the artistic director or producer and ask in a straightforward way if he approves of this direction or wants something else. Listen carefully to his concerns or objections. If you believe his ideas are worthy of consideration, discuss how your concept might change. If you need the job, you need to incorporate his ideas. Hopefully his ideas are based on experience and worthy of consideration. Keep the conversation professional and straightforward. You must stand up for your directorial vision, while remaining open to considering possible compromises. If you believe the producer's views are destructive to the play or musical, it is time to bow out of the production. However, this is a very, very hard choice to make, and carries the risk of becoming known as difficult.

Production managers often schedule and chair these meetings. Production managers and staff have rewarding but tough jobs. Remember that your job as a guest director is to inspire, engage, push, pull, and cajole **every** department to achieve the best possible production. If you find yourself being told "no" repeatedly, this can reveal one of two things: the organization is over-extended and cannot support your design, or the production manager and staff are suffering from "burnout," which has made them negative, cautious, anxious, or reluctant. When this happens in the director/designer conference, focus on the why of your concept, what's most exciting to you, and ask for creative solutions to specific artistic, technical, or design challenges of the production. Spend less time defending any one choice; rather, persuade the entire gathering to help you realize your vision. In other words, be persuasive and positive.

Onsite director/designer conferences should include touring the stage and audience space in which you will be directing. Take advantage of this opportunity to sit in seats all over the theatre, stand on stage, check the wings and the access to backstage. Ask your "tour guides" (usually production staff or stage management) how the space works in performance and what insights they have learned over time. Following the tour of the theatre, directors usually meet with each designer and staff head to talk through the entire play. When meeting with the scenic designer, technical director, and properties head, you should review the play's physical needs from the beginning to the end, describing your staging thoughts and needs for every scene and transition. Be sure to discuss each important moment in the story (e.g., Malcolm bringing in the severed head of Macbeth or how you envision approaching the flying in *Peter Pan*). The meeting may include composers, lighting and multimedia designers who will want to discuss time of day, scene changes, visual imagery, special effects, mood and atmosphere. In the meeting with the costume designer, be prepared to discuss each character (and actor, if cast), the physical action, accessories (e.g., sword belts, canes, hats, or wigs), and costume changes. For a musical, it's vital that the choreographer and music director attend the director/design conference. When meeting with the music director, you should confirm the size and instrumentation of the orchestra, the process of engaging musicians, the type of wireless microphones being used, and the location of the orchestra, speakers, mixing and sound boards, etc.

Typically, each designer meets with the production department head who is responsible for executing the designs. For instance, costume designers meet with the costume shop manager, review costume counts, check stock, and determine what will be rented, pulled or built. At the end of the day, you will usually come together again. The production manager will review the relevant dates for the first round of detailed designs, the timeframe for your responses and requests for revisions, the schedule for the theatre to compare the designs with the available human and financial resources, and negotiations if the design is over budget, and the final approvals by you, the designers, and the theatre.

If you lack experience directing in the theatre's configuration (e.g., thrust, in-the-round, audience on two sides), spend more time walking the stage, checking sightlines, and the actor/audience relationship. Ask your stage manager and production manager for observations and tips in using the space. If you need additional help, reach out to your trusted colleagues and mentors.

As a director, you will be asked to approve the designs long before rehearsals begin. This means you need to determine if the designs support your vision **and** the action of the play. You must evaluate and decide on both when you receive preliminary designs. Most scenic designers will provide you with a ground plan and sketches of the set for scenes throughout the script. If they don't, ask them to do so. The visual design of the scenery may be stunning, but does it advance the story? It's essential to take the preliminary scenic designs and work through the show at a very detailed and specific level. No one else is going to do this. Does the ground plan support the necessary exits, entrances, and playing areas? Will it support efficient and effective scenic transitions? Thoroughly check the ground plan and scenic design, including any necessary elements, such as projection screens, traps, etc. Look at the most important scenes and events in the script to verify they are included in the design. Will it work for the dramatic progression of the show? If you don't address these issues, you will spend precious time trying to make an awkward set work during tech rehearsal, which amounts to the most inefficient use of your and others' time. On the other hand, if the set is a daring and innovative use of the playing space that provides an extraordinary visual imagery that aligns with your vision and the play, persevere. Talk with your scenic designer constantly and describe any problems and concerns you are encountering. Ask him to help you create an innovative and workable plan for staging. And remember that professional actors often figure out how to use a set effectively. After considerable effort and discussion, if you continue to believe the scenery is not workable, decide what changes are needed and immediately communicate with the designer and the theatre. The amount of time you spend in reviewing the initial design will depend upon the size and scope of the musical or play, but you **must** judge how well the designs will work in advance. Again, no one else will do so.

Working from sketches and a ground plan—or if you're lucky, a model—is a skill you will need to acquire and/or develop. If you have difficulty in visualizing the staging and action from a ground plan and sketches, it's important that you work to improve. Visit the studio of a friend who is a scene designer, look at ground plans, elevations, sketches, models, and production photos from several projects. For the current production, ask your designer to help you translate the ground plan into a form that you can comprehend. If you need additional help, ask your mentor or your network of trusted colleagues for assistance. Working with a model built to scale is much easier, as long as the model also indicates the audience area. Directors who cannot envision the set until they see it onstage severely limit their careers. Very few theatres can afford or are willing to make expensive (or sometimes any) changes to a set during rehearsals or tech/dress just because a director was unable to figure out in advance the following: how the design works, how human bodies fit the stage, how scenic transitions will work, how the action will unfold, and how sightlines will remain open.

The first round of costume designs for period productions are pencil or ink sketches of the major characters in the major scenes in the play with fabric swatches or colors attached. For a contemporary show, the designer may use selected pictures and images from magazines, fashion shows, or costume history books. You must look at the entire set of sketches to determine if the visual concept or style supports your artistic vision of the show. And you must decide if individual costumes illuminate the characters in the show. Finally, check that each actor can accomplish the necessary physical action in the costume as designed. In sound and music designs, the process is typically iterative. You will receive various sound effects to try for moments in the show for your comment or approval. For music, you will receive songs, dances, or transitional pieces of music that will bridge one scene into the next. The timing of these transitional music cues will often change once you move into the theatre, so many composers send you themes and samples of varying length to build a catalog of editable cues. Listen carefully and, if appropriate, try out the sound and music cues in rehearsal.

You will need to check the effectiveness and viability of all the designs. An important question is how well do the designs work together? This can be especially challenging given the differing deadlines for the design team. You may receive scenic designs first, then costume designs a few weeks later, followed by music composed for songs and transitions, followed by property designs, and ending with sound, lighting and projection designs close to tech. Most designers are smart and communicative, but make sure that you keep in contact with each designer. You are the sole judge of the cohesion in the designs. If the set is traditional, the costumes brightly colored and contemporary, and the lighting is based on the style of film noir, that may be perfect. Or not. Your task is to work with designers to make their individual artistry complement each other and support your directorial vision. What might begin as a conversation about avoiding colors that clash with scenery and lighting often turns into a fruitful discussion about the visual impact of all design elements. I am in no way endorsing using a specific year or culture for all design choices. For example, Phyllida Lloyd's extraordinary production of Friedrich Schiller's *Mary Stuart* used design to stunning effect. The script was translated and adapted by Peter Oswald, and the production starred Harriet Walter and Janet McTeer. Queen Elizabeth and Mary, Queen of Scots were the only characters dressed in Elizabethan clothing; the many men surrounding them were dressed in dark, modern, Westminster business suits. Using minimalist sets and props and bold dramatic lighting, the production underscored and illuminated the many challenges facing these two women, who were fighting for political power amid a deeply sexist court.

Detailed designs come with lists of equipment and materials to be rented or bought which are submitted to the theatre. The production staff will cost out the production. If the designs are over budget, in materials or labor, negotiations will begin between your designers and the production staff. The designer usually contacts you regarding changes requested; if not, stay in touch with the designer and the production manager to ensure that your design priorities are kept front of mind.

Throughout the design process, keep returning to the script. Your specific knowledge of it and your attention to detail can prevent many mistakes. A common mistake occurs when a costume designer purchases fabrics that cannot be stained with liquid or stage blood. If your production of *Romeo and Juliet* emphasizes the brutal violence of the fights to underscore the shocking loss of young life, you probably want stage blood in the death of Tybalt, Mercutio, Paris, and Juliet. No matter how beautiful, if the wrong fabrics are chosen (e.g., silk), you and the theatre cannot use blood or any liquid in performance. When selected costumes are being built for your show, determine if the shops are building the costumes that best support your directorial vision. If you're directing a musical (or Shakespeare play) and you asked for follow spots, smoke/fog effects, stage blood, live fire, etc., your deep knowledge of the play will help you and your designer quickly decide on priorities: what must stay and what can be cut.

Casting and hiring

"Casting is 90 percent of a director's job" is a frequently repeated adage in theatre, television, and film. No one knows who made the observation, but many well-known directors and producers have repeated some version of it, often with a different percentage (e.g., 80 percent or 60 percent). Casting is critically important to the success of any production. Bad casting (especially in important roles) can wreck a show. Further complicating the issue is how we cast: auditions and callbacks are the most unnatural practice in the theatre. The premise that a director can effectively cast an actor for a major leading or supporting role in 2–3 sessions of 10 minutes each is almost as absurd as expecting an actor to demonstrate their talent, stage presence, acting range, and ability in those same sessions. Today's increasingly common practice of auditioning by self-made video posted online adds another layer of complexity to the task that you must master. This section explores the tools, techniques, and practices that can help you succeed at casting.

All casting is subjective, based upon some combination of your intellectual judgment, instincts, taste, and intuition. As a director, your choices are influenced by the style of acting that you prefer or that the script dictates. Is it urban, contemporary, and gritty acting with a muscular intensity, or acting that is well-crafted, moment-to-moment, nuanced, and believable without affectation or "presentational" techniques? Does the musical you are directing demand a larger-than-life, high energy, and a highly theatrical style of acting? Your casting choices must change with different projects, theatre spaces, and circumstances. As we mature, many of us become more tolerant and flexible in our views regarding "great acting" or the "best" approach to performance. Although we have deep convictions and beliefs about what constitutes great acting, we choose whom to cast based upon the title, the performance space, and the concept.

The most useful piece of advice in casting is, "cast the best actor, not the type." This means casting the most talented and skilled actor, not the actor who most resembles the look, sound, and behavior of the character. To do so, you must first define what you believe great acting is and then decide which kind of actor best serves the role and the play. For me, great actors have an uncanny ability to immerse completely in their character's journey. We forget we are watching an actor perform and respond directly to another human experiencing a moment of joy, suffering, triumph, or tragedy. In a world obsessed with celebrity, performers are categorized simplistically in two ways: (1) actors who transform themselves physically, vocally, and psychologically to convincingly play many different roles, or (2) actors with remarkable physical attributes, stage presence, charisma, and magnetism who play themselves in every role. Both can deliver captivating and thrilling performances. I was amused to discover online lists of famous actors "who play themselves" and actors "who transform themselves," published by the entertainment media outlets that breathlessly cover the film and television industries. Despite the questionable credibility of the sources, these lists were surprisingly accurate. Many of us will not work with such famous actors or personalities, but I follow the same rule. I will always choose the "transformative" actor who possesses some of the physical and emotional characteristics of the role over the actor who is a perfect match in physique, voice, and behavior, but lacks the acting chops.

Many actors and directors have asked me what I look for in auditions and callbacks. Simply put, I look for one moment when the actor "becomes" the character. He manages to connect with the role, circumstances, intellect, and emotional vulnerability of Hamlet and for a split second I believe that Hamlet is alive and standing in front of me. It's the alchemical combination of the transformational acting and deep emotional connection that interests me most. The best actor seems to unlock the character and express his deepest desires and conflicts, without "performing." This is harder to describe than it is to see in the audition room. These moments set apart the actor who inhabits the part from the actor who intellectually understands the role but cannot make the emotional connection. Every professional director will spend a large portion of their career learning how to cast. Successful casting is an art form that requires a lot of trial and error. It requires an intimate knowledge of the role, as well as listening to your intuition. Here are several considerations that will help you succeed at casting.

When casting a specific show, specify the minimum requirements the actors must have for the production and the role. For example, if you are directing *Sweeney Todd*, both Sweeney and Mrs. Lovett must possess exceptional stage presence, sophisticated knowledge and expertise in music and singing, remarkable acting chops, and physical stamina. *Sweeney Todd* resembles an opera in that it is mostly sung from a score that is highly complex and demanding; if an actor cannot sing the role of Mrs. Lovett to the satisfaction of the music director, I will drop her from consideration. If she can sing gloriously but cannot act the role to my satisfaction, I will also drop her. If the music director is passionate about using her singing voice in the show, we explore other roles she might play. With *Sweeney Todd*, the choreographer's opinion is valuable but not as critical, because it's not a dance-heavy show.

Similar casting decisions confront any director of *Romeo and Juliet*. According to the script, Juliet is fourteen and Romeo is sixteen. Very, very few 14–16-year-old actors can deliver the verse, play the innocence and infatuation of their first meeting at Capulet's Party, navigate the roller coaster of high emotions caused by the many challenges they face, and turn into the determined, young adults who commit suicide in the Capulets' Tomb. Franco Zefferelli cast Olivia Hussey (15) and Leonard Whiting (17) in his beloved movie for their youth and innocence. They were breathtakingly beautiful, innocent, and vulnerable when they met, but both actors struggled to handle the verse during the highly charged moments in later scenes. Zefferelli was forced to cut dialogue and rely upon visual moments of storytelling. Unfortunately, you don't have that option in the live theatre. These examples are a good reminder for a director to consider the entire journey of the character and not focus on the first few scenes.

The show is typically cast as the design process is going on. The theatre will schedule a casting meeting to tell you about its process of casting and hiring actors. Before that meeting, review your Character Descriptions and add any additional notes you might have based upon your growing knowledge of the play. Jot down the names of any actors who you would like to consider for each role. It might also be helpful to list any famous actors who closely resemble the characters, or who represent an acting approach you hope to see in the production. Although the theatre could never afford to hire these actors, discussing their names, talents and performances will often elicit other names of similar actors. At the casting meeting, you will be expected to talk briefly but vividly about each character, including the characteristics, talents, experience, special skills or qualities that you believe are needed to play the role. In other words, you must know each role intimately and have the ability to articulate what you need from the actor playing it. All of this information should be included in your Character Descriptions document, which will prove invaluable when you're asked to contribute to "Casting Breakdowns" for the casting director and agents. Always confirm the total count of actors budgeted for your show, and the ratio of union to non-union and local to out-of-town actors, if applicable. Inquire about the casting of children. Ask for updates on any actors who were hired or were made offers before you were hired.

The next decisions concern "Pre-casting" or "Direct Offers." These are direct offers to specific actors prior to the auditions; actors who you believe are perfect for the role and so need not audition. The artistic director may have his/her own list and you will compare them. If you both agree, a direct offer can be extended to the actor. The practice of pre-casting or making direct offers prior to auditions saves both you and the theatre significant amounts of time and energy. If you successfully cast 50 percent of the show with eight or more actors by direct offer, it will substantially reduce the expense of auditions, callbacks, etc. Often these offers will overlap with auditions. While auditioning actors for the role of King Lear, you may be waiting to hear back from a specific actor to whom the theatre has made a direct offer, or the theatre may be checking interest and availability of other actors. This process can become complicated especially if you or the theatre are offering the role to prominent actors who may not be especially willing to leave town or work for the level of pay that the theatre can afford. Each such offer and decision can take a several days or weeks; watch that you and the theatre don't fall behind in the hiring of leading roles in a timely manner. However, don't be pressured into accepting an actor who doesn't fit the role or doesn't bring the level of acting that you believe is vital. If the casting becomes protracted, be open to other options and recommendations.

When casting for a musical, ask your music director and choreographer to determine the number of chorus members, principal actors, and swings needed. Also, get their specific input on dance/movement needs and singing ranges for principals and chorus actors. Can you cover the necessary action, singing parts, and dance numbers with the size of cast budgeted? Or more often, the question is how **will** you cover the necessary action, singing parts, dance numbers with the cast you have? If you're directing a musical at a theatre that hires union actors in the US, ask the theatre to request the official Breakdown of Principal and Chorus roles from the Actors' Equity Association (AEA). The union determines the breakdown of Chorus and Principal roles based upon prior Broadway productions.

In mid-size to larger subsidized theatres, you may work with an in-house casting coordinator or director as well as a contracted casting director in New York City, London, Los Angeles, etc. In addition, some theatres retain local casting directors who manage local auditions and cast for several area theatres.

If you plan or need to double actors (i.e., when an actor plays multiple roles in a show), pull out the spreadsheet you prepared entitled Scene/ Character Breakdown. Fill in the names of performers previously hired, then use the spreadsheet to identify which actor is free (and has time to make changes in and out of costume) for the second character's scenes. Also, ask the casting staff member if the theatre uses understudies. If so, do they cover the roles from within the company or do they hire additional actors? This may affect your choices in auditions.

Weeks or even months before auditions, you will be asked for a Casting Breakdown (descriptions for all the roles being cast). Depending upon the organization's agreement with Equity or AEA, the theatre may be required to publish a list and brief description of the roles available by a certain date prior to the auditions. Often the theatre must hold a local "open call" for interested union actors or an "open call" in New York or London. For musicals, major regional theatres in the US must hold an "open" call for both Principal Roles and Chorus/Ensemble Roles as part of their official auditions in New York, Chicago, Los Angeles, etc. The theatre will provide the casting director with the necessary information regarding dates, contract type, and so on.

For the Casting Breakdown you should include the role, the type of actor (e.g., leading man, character actor, ingenue); age range (i.e., the approximate age the character needs to "look" onstage; due to age discrimination laws, you cannot ask an actor his age), gender, ethnicity, special skills needed for the role, and any doubling. For musicals, you add the singing range and parts (i.e., second tenor) and dance or movement skills (e.g., Tap, Hip Hop, Ballroom) required. However, the most important information will be your description of each role. Bear in mind the audience for these descriptions: the casting director, agents or managers who represent the actors, and the actors themselves. Most casting directors will have read the script or have seen other productions. Many agents and managers will not have done so. In addition, remember that all casting directors, agents, and managers are juggling multiple jobs and clients. Casting directors are often very busy, casting theatre shows, TV/cable programs or films, and agents may represent dozens of performers and artists. You need to speak to them directly and forcefully. In my experience, the more specific your description, the better. These are **not** academic or literary descriptions, but brief, bold and vivid descriptions of what you want. Include any specific directives regarding non-traditional, diverse, differently abled, gender neutral casting, but make clear if you want to audition these actors or if you will only cast the role with one of these actors.

Your next task is to pick "Sides" for the actors to read in auditions and callbacks for each role or line of roles. Rule of thumb: initial audition readings are often scheduled in 10-minute blocks. Pick a **portion** of a scene or two that shows you the role at key moments. This is an easy task if the character only appears in a few scenes, but much harder if you're casting a major role such as Rose Maxton, Mama Nadi, Medea, Hedda Gabler, Mother Courage, or Cleopatra. Keep in mind that, generally, you will have only one reader in the room. Don't torment either the actor or the reader by picking crowd scenes. If the role is small, pick another role to use in the audition. For callbacks, pick a third speech or scene that rounds out what you need to see from the actor.

If you are using a specific edition of a play which has many versions/editions (e.g., *Look Back in Anger, The Crucible, Tartuffe*), or any play in translation or adaptation, note the edition on the Casting Breakdown. Better still, send or ask the theatre to send copies of pages of the sides from the correct script directly to the casting director, who can post them online or forward them to the agents. This avoids wasting time in auditions. Additionally, you cut lines or speeches of other characters in advance if they aren't important to the role but take care that you don't delete information that the character needs to hear within a scene. You're looking not only for the actor's interpretation, but their ability to react in the moment.

Next, send a list of actors you would like to see in auditions to both the theatre and the casting director. This list may include "courtesy auditions" for an actor out of respect for their past work with you or the theatre, but doubt that he or she will be cast. Try to keep the courtesy audition list short.

Working with casting directors

As you would expect, casting directors vary widely in personality, artistic taste, temperament, and professional knowledge. As you gain experience, remember those you find most effective. Many are smart, efficient, and capable. But like directors, some are condescending, cynical, and negative. Some seem to dislike actors, in a glib, gossipy fashion. This may reveal burnout in a very taxing profession or an underlying pessimism because of their unfulfilled aspirations. Take note of the ones who love actors, see lots of theatre, and are eager to discover new talent.

Many casting directors will aim to finish the casting as soon as possible. This is understandable, because most casting directors are retained on a flat fee that covers casting of a pre-determined number of roles. Also, casting directors usually have favorite actors and favorite agents with whom they work. They also know (or assume they know) which actors will "go out of town" and/or which will work for the weekly salary being offered. Keep in mind that good casting directors are founts of information about actors, and know their best performances, rehearsal habits, behavioral problems, and strengths and weaknesses. Many will have cast the actor in other shows at other theatres and seen his work. When casting professional child actors, casting directors and their staffs are keenly attuned to the behavior of the actor, but also to any overbearing or unpleasant behavior from the parents. Casting directors can also be an invaluable resource for discovering young adult actors, because they make a habit of attending the showcases of good conservatories to find the most promising graduates.

If you know the actor, make sure she knows that you/the theatre strongly wants her to "read" for the role or that you/the theatre has made an offer. It's sad to say, but agents and managers sometimes will not tell the actor of specific interest or even an offer, because they want the actor to stay in London or New York to be available for more lucrative work. Don't insert yourself between the representative and the actor, but make certain the actor knows.

Auditions

For auditions, the people in the room include the director, the casting director (and perhaps an assistant), the artistic director or his representative, and a reader. For a musical, add a choreographer, a music director, and an accompanist. For a new play or musical, add the playwright or the composer, lyricist, and book writer. The director sets the atmosphere of the room. I ask the casting director or assistant to announce the actor's name and role being read as he enters. I verbally greet the actor to establish a welcoming space for the actor and attempt to relieve any overwrought nerves. As the director, I also introduce who is in the room, including the reader. If you don't want to do this, ask the casting director to do so.

As the actor and reader confer, scan the actor's picture and resumé, from a stack which is usually given to you at the beginning of the day. Quickly check and note several things:

- Does their headshot match how they look? If not, jot down the differences.
- Check the kind of roles they have previously played, and the directors and the theatres they've worked with, their training, and any special skill directly applicable to this role.

This is very quick. If you don't have time, do it later. Give the actor permission to begin, with an affirmative head nod or say "when you're ready . . ."

Watch the audition attentively. During the reading, some directors take copious notes and some take none. I use a personal shorthand to take brief notes about acting ability, physical capabilities, vocal skills, interpretation, emotional connection and more. Given the number of actors who audition for each production, I find these notes invaluable in remembering specific impressions about the actor and his reading. Use or create a system of note taking that works for you.

If I'm interested in the actor after the first reading, I always ask for an adjustment in a short, select portion of the scene or speech. This is an important litmus test for me. It often reveals if the actor is unwilling or inflexible to change his interpretation. I don't judge the effectiveness of the actor's adjustment, but rather watch his receptivity to direction and his eagerness to "try a new idea." If he will not attempt it or clearly doesn't want to make a change, I eliminate him from consideration. Beyond testing the actor's willingness to take direction and try a different approach, his reaction also reveals if he's listening to you and willing to "play." I resist a lot of questions from the actor, such as requests for direction or extended discussion before the reading. I want to see the actor's initial understanding and interpretation of the role. However, if multiple actors are misunderstanding a role or the style of a play, I will give brief notes to the actor before he or she begins reading. This often happens with new plays or works set in unusual cultures. During the session, the artistic director, the casting director and I quickly divide the actors into three piles: actors to callback, actors we may want to callback, and actors of no interest. If the actor is very good, but not appropriate for this project, I notate my interest in seeing them for future shows. After their reading, I thank each actor for their audition and say goodbye. As they leave, I jot down any additional notes, including any perception of a difficult personality or attitude problem.

Beginning early in the audition schedule, take any available time between auditions to discuss actors of strong and moderate interest to you with the artistic director or theatre's representative and with the casting director. This conversation can reveal similarities or differences in taste or opinion between you and the artistic director. It also can tell you if you're not seeing the best group of actors for a particular role. The casting director can also provide useful information on the actor, such as noting that his audition was "uncharacteristically poor" or not. He can also provide information on the actor's reputation and work ethic.

As a director, I keep watching the clock. I use all the time I can for actors of great interest, but also try to respect the time of all the actors waiting. As auditions and callbacks proceed, I will learn a lot about each role, each scene, and the script. Although I might think that my character descriptions were brilliant and complete, actually seeing and hearing the actors will always illuminate and clarify what I want in each role and in each scene, and often in the entire production. Jot down these observations as they occur.

Whenever there is a lull in auditions, review your notes and flip through the resumés and pictures. This proves enormously helpful in remembering each performer and his work, but it also aids in starting lists of callbacks and "maybe" callbacks. Casting is exciting and exhausting and taking cogent, clear notes proves invaluable when you come to make final decisions after several days. If you are casting with other directors for multiple productions in rep or in a festival format, your notes become even more crucial. Often there will be serious horse trading to finalize casting, to ensure that each show gets strong actors for its leading roles; directing in rep usually requires compromises in supporting and smaller roles. If you are casting from large, open calls, your notes become indispensable. Finally, your notes will be useful when and if you need to replace an actor. Between the time of auditions and callbacks, actors may receive another offer that is more attractive, such as a West End show, a television/cable series or a film role that provides much better pay (sometimes by multiples of what the theatre can afford to pay), a longer gig, or an opportunity to act for a much larger audience. An actor also may have a family or personal emergency, etc. The fastest way to re-cast is to check your detailed audition notes to determine if the next actor down the list is a good choice.

At the end of each day, review the list of those actors called back and decide what to do about the "maybe callback" actors. If you want a specific actor to audition for a different role, ask the casting director to check the actor's interest and to call her back. You or the theatre may use a "direct to callback" practice, in which an actor skips the auditions and attends the callbacks. These actors are generally very experienced, well known, or those with whom you (or the theatre) have worked and are confident of their likely strength in the role. "Direct to callback" is a good tool and it can save time and relieve stress, but use it with thought and discretion. Once your list of callbacks is confirmed, the casting director will set them up. Before callbacks begin, take the time to review the relevant resumés and pictures more carefully.

Finally, when casting an actor for the first time in a demanding role, **always** contact any references you can, such as directors or artistic directors of theatres at which he has worked. Ask about his acting talent, appropriateness for the role, work ethic, willingness to collaborate, and professional attitude.

Callbacks

Callbacks are invaluable. They present you with a chance to refresh your memory and re-evaluate what each actor brings to the role. More importantly, the length of a callback is typically longer than the first reading, giving you time to work with the actor, give notes and adjustments, and observe their emotional and psychological connections to the work. You can also sense their temperament and willingness to collaborate. Callbacks are often indispensable in making better decisions in casting. Although I might believe one actor is the best choice for a leading role from auditions, the callback often changes my mind. Remember that you probably have better knowledge of the role, because you've watched several actors have a crack at it in initial auditions. Through auditions, you will have refined who the character is for you and what you will need from the actor. In addition, callbacks may give you the chance to mix and match actors and watch their interpersonal chemistry and connection. As you gain more experience in callbacks, you will begin to tailor your notes to the individual actor, trying to bring out what you most need to see from him. In practice, the art of casting is based on your instinct and intuition and the skill in giving a note that elicits a new layer of emotional and intellectual connection between the actor and his role.

For example, the melancholic Jaques in *As You Like It* is a very difficult role to cast. He fashions himself as a sophisticated, melancholic, intellectually brilliant philosopher with a biting, censorious wit. He literally wants to criticize the world without consequence. The Duke debates and satirizes Jaques, and both Orlando and Rosalind beat him at games of wit. He's pretentious, elitist, affected, and cynical. Many an actor wants to approach the character in absolutes. Either he's a tragic figure at the center of a corrupt and despairing world of betrayal or he's an affected fop, slinging witticisms and nailing other characters in their stupidity from love or ignorance. It's a remarkably difficult character to direct (and act), and directors often choose to encourage the pessimistic, dark brilliance of his intellect or encourage the humorous, pretentious, licentious, but highly satiric aristocrat. In my view, he's a mixture of both. If you examine his dramatic function in the play, he appears to be the Dark Fool to Touchstone's Light Fool.

Many of us are forced to learn Jacque's famous speech, *The Seven Ages of Man*, early in our education in appreciation of Shakespeare's description of the stages of human life. However, in context, this speech betrays a deep pessimism about existential doom facing mankind, as we progress from mewling and puking baby to helpless, incapacitated, agèd child. In auditioning for this part, a brilliant, deeply experienced actor (he had played every comic role in Shakespeare), gave the speech with tour-de-force comic timing. At callbacks, I suggested that the speech progressed from satiric joking as a boy reluctantly going to school to Jacques' ultimate fear of dementia or Alzheimer's Disease. For an intellectual and philosopher, I could not imagine a worse fate than losing one's mind. The actor began with the same comic verse, but step-by-step descended into a bitter, chilling, and deeply moving conclusion. My note was not detailed or analytical, but the actor found his way through the speech with a new purpose. This example brings up another adage for auditions and callbacks: don't over-explain or talk for too long. Callbacks are not about your directorial brilliance, they are about evoking something new and different from the actor.

Making decisions, making offers

At the end of callbacks, you will be asked to decide on casting. Review each actor who was called back and then rank them in order of preference for each role. If the artistic director, theatre's casting person, or producer is in the room, this can become an extended discussion or heated debate before you come to an agreement on the list. If no one is representing the organization at callbacks, the lists for each role, with pictures, resumés and your preferences attached, are sent for approval. At this time, some casting directors will push you to decide quickly and make offers, wanting to complete the process. You can and should resist this pressure. Take a couple of days to decide. If you are undecided about certain actors, you should think about matching and mixing actors in the company. Or perhaps you need to wait to hear from a significant reference. This is a gut check moment, too. If the theatre or the casting office is pressing you hard to cast an actor who you don't feel is right for any role, take the time to figure out why you are hesitating. Whenever I have taken the advice of someone else in the room against my own instincts and judgment, the choice has always come back to haunt me.

A difficult situation arises whenever an artistic director's or producer's taste is markedly different to yours. Be alive to this during initial auditions, callbacks, and responses to your list of offers. No matter how difficult it gets, don't give in, especially on major roles. Don't say no, but rather start a discussion. Focus on the "positives and negatives" of the actor's audition, talent, and work. Discuss the traits, styles, and kind of actor you think best serves the role. Listen carefully and consider their comments. Then speak your mind. Hopefully, you will come to a workable understanding. However, do remember that, in professional theatres or commercial organizations, the artistic leader or producer has final casting or hiring approval. If it's a new play or musical, the creators must also approve.

There are some actors who will prove unsatisfactory, problematic or worse during rehearsals. Each of us will make these casting mistakes at some point in our careers. These actors often attract our strong interest or fascinate us in auditions for one reason or another, but knowing some of the common types will help you remain objective in considering them. These include:

- The actor whose best performance is her audition. A few actors are brilliant at auditioning, but less effective at crafting or creating a full performance. This is hard to recognize, but the casting director may know more. Check references.
- The actor who cannot learn his lines. This is very difficult to ascertain in an audition. Check **recent** jobs and call references, especially if the role is large and demanding.

- The oppositional or confrontational actor. If the actor protests, argues with or questions every note you give him, don't hire him.
- The narcissistic actor. Observe how the actor connects or doesn't with the reader. Evaluate how the actor responds to your notes and direction. Listen for the way they speak about the character and the play. Is it perceptive and heartfelt? Or do they refer back to their insights, deep experience or superior acting talent? When in doubt, check references.
- The actor who matches your personal ideal of beauty, charisma, gender, sex appeal, and personality. Step back and ask the others in the room for their frank opinion of the actor's work and talent.
- The actor who knows how to praise, flatter, and boost your ego. Same as above.
- The actor who has performed the role or show several times (especially in commercial productions) and "knows how the role (and show) should be performed." As a rule, I try not to hire these actors, as they may stifle the choices by other actors or resist changes to their performance. If you are interested, give big adjustments or out-of-the-box changes during auditions and callbacks. See how they respond.
- An actor who doesn't seem up to the physical challenges of the role. Incorporate physical activity into the callback scene.
- An actor who cannot handle the words, ideas, wit and intellect of a heightened language play, such as those written by Tom Stoppard. Give him detailed vocal, thought and text notes. Ask the others in the room how well they could understand and follow the ideas of the actor.

If you sense any of these issues during casting, you have two excellent resources: (1) the artistic director and casting director sitting in the room with you, and (2) the directors or theatres that have hired the actor in the recent past. Ask for their frank observations and opinions of the performer, based upon their experience. However, remember that there are always two sides to any conflict or controversy; don't let one opinion change your decision to hire or not hire an actor.

Finally, if you find yourself ignoring actors from diverse backgrounds, recognize that. This is your problem, not the actors'. Confront your bias and take workshops or classes on conscious and unconscious discrimination. Re-examine your discomfort or disapproval. Attend as many shows as you can with diverse actors in a variety of roles.

Theatres or producers handle the process of making offers to agents in different ways. Once the artistic director or producer has signed off on casting, the managing director or general manager will make the offer and negotiate the contract. Occasionally the casting director will make the offer and negotiate the contract.

Whatever you do, keep the appointment schedule of auditions, and always ask for pictures and resumés of all the actors of interest from callbacks and auditions but, most of all, **keep all of your notes**. These will be invaluable if you "lose an actor." When I last directed *Hamlet*, I hired a gifted, charismatic, and highly skilled actor to play the leading role. He pulled out of the show for a longer and higher profile job shortly before the first rehearsal. I looked through my notes and files of resumés and pictures and selected a few actors. When we checked interests and availability, none were free. Then I remembered a remarkable video audition for the role. Although I had never met this actor, much less directed him, I found several positive notes from past performances of his that I had seen. After checking a couple of references, I called the actor immediately to see if he was still interested and available. He was, and I hired him on the spot. He proved to be a much better, more experienced, and versatile actor for Hamlet than my first choice. Again, keep your notes.

5

Rehearsals in the Studio

Before rehearsals begin

The week before rehearsals begin, I reach out to my Stage Manager (SM). If the theatre hires union actors, the stage manager will be a member of the same union. Stage managers serve several masters: (1) the union—the SM is charged with enforcing the union's contractual work rules and policies, (2) the theatre—the SM is a manager within the production department, and (3) you, the director—the SM will assist in guiding the show towards your artistic vision. She will run the rehearsals, call required breaks, work from your proposed rehearsal schedule to incorporate costume fittings, stage combat rehearsals, and more. Stage managers set up rehearsals for children in the cast, work with parents, and schedule any additional calls (such as music, choreography, voice/dialect, or movement rehearsals), arrange meetings with production heads and shops, and handle any other requests from marketing, development or other departments. It's a great benefit to you if she has worked at this theatre prior to your show, either as a resident or guest stage manager. If so, she will have an established relationship with the organization and knows the best ways to achieve the best results.

Establishing a positive, open, and trusting relationship with the stage manager is invaluable. She is the primary communicator with the rest of the organization. She knows information that may not have been communicated to you, such as dates of the "designer run-through," how the theatre expects the tech/dress process to run, how photo calls and press/media calls function, which department heads in production/tech need specific direction and which are experienced and proactive, and so on. After opening night, the stage manager is responsible for maintaining the performance by giving notes to actors, crew, and house management. The best stage managers are excellent communicators and know when notes should be delivered in person, in private, by phone or intercom, or by email or text.

My initial conversation with the stage manager is very important. It will cover many subjects, but focuses on a detailed review of the entire rehearsal schedule. This lets me decide in advance how much time I will use for each part of the process (i.e., read-through, blocking, scene work, run-throughs, tech, dress, preview, and opening rehearsals). We set target dates for completing each part. We also review the theatre's practices or expectations for the first day of rehearsal, including the read-through. I ask who attends first rehearsal (usually the designers, the artistic director, and staff, but often many others including the production manager and heads, the managing director, marketing and development staff, donors or show sponsors, volunteers, coaches or specialists, and more). We plan this day accordingly, and I discuss my goals for the call. When needed, I review new line assignments or cuts, and stage directions that I want read at the first read-through. If the production is blessed with a dramaturg, we talk about how much time he will spend in rehearsal and how and when he can share his research packet. Typically, the costume shop will request short sessions with actors new to the theatre for measurements and, of course, the actors must elect a union deputy. The deputy serves as a liaison between the actors and the union, and fills out various reports weekly. We look at important dates (e.g., when the artistic director attends rehearsals, the dates of the production meetings, designer run-throughs, any pre-arranged conflicts such as when an actor or designer has been given contractual permission to miss a rehearsal or performance (which should have been approved by you in advance if it affects rehearsal), and the process of moving onstage, tech/dress, previews, and opening. I also ask about the theatre's practices and policies on learning lines and any relevant or unusual union work rules or policies that will affect rehearsals.

If my production is set in an "historical period and/or foreign location," I ask the stage manager to immediately request rehearsal clothes that can be pulled from stock, such as skirts and blouses, corsets, leather jackets and overcoats, shoes, hats, canes, weapons (props) and their holders (costumes), as well as knee or elbow pads, mats for stage combat, highly physical scenes, etc. As mentioned earlier, I use the term "historical period and/or foreign location" loosely, referring to any period more than 25–30 years in the past. These rehearsal items are enormously helpful to actors; a "pulled from stock" blouse and skirt, suit jacket, or period footwear can radically change an actor's physical approach to the role and saves time later when the costumes and props arrive. I ask for these items as early as possible, hoping they can be pulled during the first costume fittings before the blocking begins.

The night before the first rehearsal, I review the photos and resumés of each performer in the show as well as my notes from auditions and callbacks. If I'm missing any materials, I ask the theatre's casting contact for the missing resumés or bios and headshots in advance.

When I am directing out-of-town, I ask the theatre to let me arrive a couple of days early. This gives me time to learn the city and theatre I'm working in, fetch groceries, and settle in. I can also meet the company manager, staff of the theatre, and tour the facility, especially the stage and the rehearsal hall. A guest director also may need to sign paperwork, and get an ID. But my most urgent task is meeting with stage management.

As your freelance jobs grow each year, preparation for upcoming shows requires increased organization and discipline. This is crucial, because your time becomes very crunched. Your one day off each week may be consumed by flying elsewhere for auditions or design conferences. Or you may spend the day working on the script and designs for future shows, not to mention the show you're currently rehearsing. In addition, you will want to connect with your significant other or family, take care of personal needs, and handle any delayed correspondence or communication. With rehearsal six days a week, it's also vitally important for you to take time to recharge your batteries in whatever way you enjoy.

The first rehearsal

The first rehearsal is an exciting, informative, and stressful occasion for a director. It's jam-packed. Many theatres hold a "meet and greet" for actors, stage management, production staff, marketing, administrative staff, volunteers, donors, etc. When the first rehearsal begins, I ask everyone in the room to introduce themselves and say what role or function each has on the show or within the organization. If it's a new play, I then ask the playwright to speak about how and where the idea for the play emerged, and what she hopes we can achieve in its premiere. However, be aware that some playwrights prefer not to speak at this time.

The next step is the Director's Introductory Talk. Directors are expected to present their directorial vision for the play in an inspiring, dynamic, and engaging manner. This includes telling the assembled company what you would like to achieve and how you intend to get there. I encourage every director to include any personal responses to the script, such as what makes the play inspiring, emotionally moving, engaging, and appealing to you. Include your thoughts on why this play is especially relevant and timely. Avoid talking too long, lecturing, or trying to demonstrate how brilliant your vision is. Wrap up by describing briefly the physical world of the play by giving an overview of the major ideas that you and your designers have used in creating that world. Then hand over the meeting to the designers to share their creative work on the play to date.

Each will discuss his or her artistic approach to the show, using examples from the designs and/or research. Scenic designers present their work in sketches, paint elevations, photos of research, ground plans, and white or painted scale models of the set. She talks through the major scenes, using sketches or scene changes in the model. Costume designers often share costume sketches with color and fabric swatches for classics or shows with more elaborate costumes. For contemporary or modern dress shows, they often share a collage of clippings, magazine photos, fashion shoots, or quick sketches for each character derived from research and meetings with the director. Most costumers present their designs as works in progress, knowing that specific choices may change given each performer's body type, their character's physical action, and the actor's personal opinions about the character or sometimes their physique. The final design will emerge from conversations between you, the actor, and the designer. If you perceive consternation from a specific actor, note it. Later, you can ask the stage manager to include you in any fittings for that actor. If you haven't worked with either the costume designer or the performers, ask to attend a fitting for costumes of the principal actors.

The presentations of the other designers will depend upon the progress of each design element by the first rehearsal. For example, the multimedia/projection designer may show some preliminary imagery, and the composer may play samples of music. The sound designer may discuss his approach to sound cues (e.g., realistic, atmospheric, non-naturalistic, a soundscape based on the leading role's perception of the world, live or recorded). If a designer is not present, the director or a production staff member will address that design. When working in a larger theatre that can afford coaches and specialists (e.g., voice, speech and dialect; fight director; dramaturg, movement specialist), I ask them to introduce themselves and briefly talk about their approaches to the show in rehearsals.

For musicals, the first day of rehearsals is very different. To accomplish a read-through of a musical without singing the songs is awkward and counterproductive. After all, the cast needs time to learn the music. The most common practice is to schedule the director/design presentation on the first gathering of the full company but then hold the read-through/sing-through a few days later. The exception may be a new musical when the composer or music director wishes to play and sing through the score at the first rehearsal. Otherwise, the first few days of rehearsal are spent learning the music, song by song. As that proceeds, the choreographer begins dance rehearsals (also dependent on the actors knowing the music). The first read-through/sing-through is far more effective and useful once the actors are familiar with the score.

The first read-through

The first read-through is a nerve-wracking event for most actors and directors. A two-time Tony Award-winning actor recently told me, "I've been hired to play the role, I know that I have the job, and I'm prepared for rehearsal, but I can't help feeling that I need to prove myself worthy of the role in the first read-through." Before the initial read-through, I try to remove the expectation of "performance" by asking the company to use the opportunity to talk and listen to each other and hear the play aloud. It's important to address up front any uses of dialect, pronunciation of names, locations or unusual terms, as well as cuts or line assignments not yet made.

For dialect and pronunciations, I often suggest the actors make their best guesses or attempts if they feel confident to do so. If not, read the play in their personal dialect. Finally, clarify how you have asked the stage manager to read the stage directions.

Listen and watch the read-through without taking a lot of small, detailed notes. If anyone is talking too softly, call it out. Although this is not a performance, it's also not a time to hide. Don't stop the reading for notes or comments, unless something goes significantly awry. Keep your focus on how the play unfolds, how each actor is initially responding to his role, and consider which actors, scenes or moments may need additional guidance. Jot down what surprises you, good or bad, but the main thing is to watch and listen attentively. At the end of the reading, applaud and thank the cast, and call for a break. Ask your stage manager for the reading time, though know that the actual production will likely take much longer. Check in with your creative team for questions or concerns.

After the read-through, I make a few observations to the company. I point out moments, scenes, lines or action that connect to the vision of the play I am pursuing. Then I encourage actors to ask questions if they didn't understand a major reference, line or plot development, and finally, I open up the discussion to the assembled company. I encourage everyone to speak about moments or scenes that were surprising, moving, meaningful, exciting or especially powerful. Finally, I discuss what we will be working on during the next few days. The first rehearsal is often an adrenaline-infused experience, with high spirits, expectations, and nerves. Some of what a director says will not fully register, but everyone will "survive" the first read-through! And all of us want to move on and begin working on the play.

Every director faces a period of proving herself to the cast; you will need to "win the room." Consciously or not, every cast wants reassurance in your capabilities as a director. When I was freelance directing, I dreamed that this "testing" of my direction in early rehearsals would disappear once I led a theatre. Alas, not so. I now believe that it's a natural part of the process of directing. Working at the same theatre and with same cast or creative staff shortens the period of testing, but it's still present. If you are well-prepared; if you can inspire, motivate, passionately persuade, and stir the hearts and minds of the company; and if do your job well in early rehearsals, this testing naturally disappears. However, you should expect to have to explain, discuss, rephrase, and restate your vision many, many times.

Table work

Typically, the next few rehearsals are devoted to "table work." The director and (if you have one) the dramaturg or voice/text coach will work through the play line by line, scene by scene, and act by act with the cast. Table work (sometimes called "text work") can be highly effective as a guided, collaborative, and communal process of discovery. It can include running down the specific meaning of lines, researching cultural references, script analysis, and exploring the given circumstances and context. For the director, it's a valuable opportunity to guide the actors towards specific interpretations of their characters, based upon your artistic vision. For the company, the work can identify and clarify the progression of the story, reveal ideas and themes that run through the play, and provide insight into any historical, cultural or social behaviors and beliefs that inform the world of the play. If you take advantage of this time, it becomes a highly engaging process for you and the actors during which you can start to explore each character's specific motivations, conflicts, and relationships, as well as the arc of each character's journey. Traditionally, the entire cast is called for table work, which lets each actor hear the references to their role in other scenes, but most importantly, uncovers the issues, words, themes, and ideas that repeatedly emerge from the writing.

When directing Shakespeare, classics or plays with heightened language, table work also becomes the time to explore the specific meaning, context, rhetorical structure, and progression of the verse or prose. Many directors and actors fail at Shakespeare, because they have only a generalized comprehension of the words, lines, speeches, and scenes. They know what the speech is generally "about," but they don't know the specific meaning of each word, or line, and they don't recognize the density of thought, metaphor, and emotion found in verse. Until the language is thoroughly investigated, it's very difficult to make Shakespeare's verse immediate and active from the beginning of a speech until the end.

However, it's essential to keep your table work productive and moving forward. If it begins to bog down in extended conversation or the voicing of personal opinions (especially from cast members in smaller roles), or moves sideways into topics that are not relevant, it's your job to redirect it. Table work can be a delightful period of exploration, discovery, and direction. It often sets the tone for the remainder of the work in the rehearsal hall. However, don't make the mistake of believing every professional actor enjoys or wants to spend time on table work. Some want to move directly to staging and others wisely resist talking too much about their personal approach to a character. They prefer to delve deeply into the character and the acting during blocking and scene work. Other actors arrive impressively prepared, having pored over the script prior to rehearsal, which is admirable as long as they haven't already decided on their performance. Some actors love to spend hours talking about the script, the characters, and the ideas, before moving on to blocking. Either extreme can become tedious or enervating. Set the expectations up front to use the process you deem best. And pay attention to the time you are spending around the table.

Blocking rehearsals

As mentioned in the previous chapter, one of the best ways to evaluate the effectiveness of a scene design is to pre-block the production at a detailed level before approval. Pull out your notes and use them. Prepare well for blocking and staging rehearsals. Review the approved designs for scenery, traps, flying scenery, furniture, and props for each scene. Using this information, work through your production book again in a detailed manner, including entrances and exits, the flow of scenes, and find the best progression of staging through the play.

Prior to the blocking rehearsal for each scene, prepare the physical action in detail for the actors. For your first professional productions, use the tools you have learned to stage both the overall action of each scene as well as the specific physical movements of each character. As you become more confident and experienced, you will find that you won't need to block so much in advance. However, for multi-scene, large cast shows, you should have a well-prepared plan of blocking.

If you haven't developed the skill to use the ground plan or model for staging, ask to use the studio prior to rehearsal calls to work through each scene. Creating or reviewing the blocking with your assistant, a production assistant or a volunteer in the rehearsal room is valuable, because you can judge quickly if your mental assumptions of the size and layout of the set are correct or out-of-scale. If you are seriously pressed for rehearsal time (e.g., in stock or festival theatres), your blocking needs to be very well-planned in advance, so that you can stage the scenes quickly and efficiently, while expecting the actors to solve details of blocking and action. Remember, the actors (and sometimes the stage manager) can often come up with better blocking than yours.

For most of us, the blocking of the first scenes and/or the first large scenes will take longer, as we figure out how to use the space. No matter how well you've sketched out the scenes in your head, you will likely be surprised. However, as you become familiar with the set, the actors, and the script, you will gain speed. In my view, blocking and staging are inter-related, but different. Blocking refers to the physical actions and movements of the actors, based on the intentions of the characters in the scene. This requires a director to approach each role with an empathetic understanding while keeping in mind the role's function within the play. "Staging" deals with storytelling, the progression of the physical action, composition and focus, and the overall journey of the play. Sometimes derided in contemporary theatre as old-fashioned or artificial, stage picture or composition is a potent and useful skill. Stage picture is another level of the structure, form, or design of storytelling. It is the technique used to focus and highlight key moments in the story. When composition is executed with skill and art, it subtly underscores and enhances the artistic vision of a production. The best directors use composition to create a remarkable flow and vividness for a play. This, in turn, often means that they have an easier and more effective transition to the theatre space, because they rarely mistake the amount of room the human bodies need in space or where the audience should be looking, even without the considerable help of the lighting design.

Actors respond eagerly to effective blocking, because it physically grounds, supports and clarifies their work. I change the blocking frequently, trying different approaches to scenes and moments. Although I rely upon considerable input, conversation, and suggestions from the actors (who often solve these problems brilliantly after I lay out the vision for a scene), I also give them time to write down the blocking during the rehearsal, and, time permitting, we review the blocking before moving on to the next scene. First blocking rehearsals should provide a sturdy, workable foundation for the action of the scene, while helping each individual actor find his character's physical journey. While I firmly believe that the professional actor is responsible for motivating any blocking or acting choice given by the director, blocking works best when the process is a collaborative discovery of the physical and psychological action.

Early career directors often have trouble judging the amount of time they will need to block. This can push them towards two extremes. They can rush through the blocking without giving the actor an explanation (i.e., the "why") for the blocking. They don't answer the questions from actors regarding motivation or the purpose of specific movements and physical actions.

These directors often become fixated on their pre-planned blocking and refuse to consider ideas and contributions from the actors which would help to improve blocking or solve challenges. At its worst, this approach treats actors like moveable objects, rather than human beings. There are several reasons a director may rush: some become panicked by the limited amount of time to block the play and others believe their blocking must be executed first without question. Many directors hurtle through blocking, because they consciously or unconsciously need reassurance that their staging will "work" for the entire show. If taken to an extreme, these directors schedule a run-through within a couple days of beginning blocking. There are several warning signs when the process is too rushed: some actors complain that they (as the characters) "don't know what they're doing"; and other actors cannot remember the blocking or the lines. This reveals a critical, missing gap in the process—the actors haven't had time to connect their words to their actions and blocking.

The opposite extreme is spending too much time on blocking, thereby shortening the time for scene work, run-throughs, tech, and dress. This approach can become very frustrating for the actors, as it increases the time between rehearsals of each scene. In my experience, directors who take too much time to block are often inadequately prepared or, even worse, they are waiting for the actors to block the play. The first is wasting time, the second is avoiding directing. Both are unprofessional. Expecting the actors to "block scenes" is asking for trouble. One or two actors will take over the process and conflicts will inevitably emerge. In the absence of a foundational staging structure, actors will often push or create performances that are overly intense or highly elaborate.

Either of these approaches reveals a lack of leadership from a director. He may not know what he wants, is intimidated by the performers or the script, or avoids making decisions by promoting an overly collaborative and inclusive process. This last approach may reveal a director's psychological need to make everyone feel "included, valued or happy." This is ironic, because a director wanting a conflict-free room will often create conflicts by letting everyone have a voice, while never making a firm decision about what's best for the show.

The pressures of directing at a much higher level in the profession can lead a director to take a more passive role in rehearsal. When I assisted Michael Langham on *Henry IV, Part 1* at The Stratford Festival, he was suddenly hospitalized after four days of rehearsals. I had been hired at the last minute, and I knew the play, but had never worked on it. When it became clear that Langham would not return for a few weeks, I was thrust into blocking the show. I knew how to block a Shakespeare play reasonably well and had prepared effective and specific blocking for the play. In the rehearsal hall, however, I was intimidated by the remarkable talent and experience of the actors, and retreated to reverential collaboration, suggesting blocking rather than specifying it. Most of the actors were supportive and helpful once they saw that my suggestions worked well. However, the actor playing Falstaff was not, because he believed that he should have been appointed the director, too. Blocking rehearsals descended into chaos whenever Falstaff was part of a scene. Ignoring the rolled eyes and grunts of disapproval by the other actors, the actor resisted any direction, stating, "I don't know if Michael [Langham] would want me to do that." After a few days of trying to "collaborate" with him, I had to change my approach. Finally, I publicly confronted him and demanded that he follow my direction until Langham returned (which would not happen until final dress). He walked out of rehearsal. The next day, he returned to tell me I had finally taken control, and he respected that. He appreciated the blunt and strong approach I had taken. The remarkable actor Nicholas Pennell leaned over to me during a break and said, "Bravo! Remember that all actors need and want good direction, no matter how big a 'talent' we are—or think we are!"

If you find yourself stuck or indecisive, work out your blocking for a scene **before** you judge it wrong or inadequate. At the same time, instruct the company that you expect them to try the blocking first and discuss later. Give yourself and the company less time for consideration or debate and more time for experimentation and moving forward. Also, in such a situation, it's good to talk through your blocking/staging issues with your stage manager or assistant. As a final resort, contact a trusted colleague or your mentor. The act of succinctly explaining a thorny staging problem to someone else often leads you to discover new solutions with a freedom and clarity hard to find during the pressures of rehearsal.

Managing the room and setting expectations

While stage managers "call and run" each rehearsal, the director must "manage the room." Simply put, you must create the working atmosphere that you want in the rehearsal room. Managing the room also means managing the many different personalities, egos, talents, and approaches to acting in the company, while establishing a productive, safe environment for actors to explore choices. There are as many successful approaches to managing the room as there are personalities of directors. The continuum ranges from dictatorial control to waiting to see what the "actor brings to the role" and then selecting what works. Directors can be intellectually brilliant but emotionally disconnected; voluble, passionate, and charismatic; generous and empathetic to the actors' journeys; demanding and distant; work instinctually or intuitively; or eschew specific direction in favor of wide-ranging discussions. Directors of classics and musicals may choose to begin rehearsals with prescribed warm-ups; others might use improvization, exercises or theatre games to begin rehearsal; and still others like to begin the day with casual conversations. The best directors do not embrace extremes. They sense what needs to happen with the performers in the room and use whatever tactic, technique, or practice works best; and they adapt their approach to the situation and the script. These leaders also react consistently and thoughtfully, and don't allow themselves displays of volatility, negativity, frustration or blame.

When I visited rehearsals of a Broadway-bound show, directed by famed film and stage director Mike Nichols, I was taken aback by the daily practice of beginning every rehearsal with a 30-minute conversation filled with backstage stories, gossip, and theatrical "war stories." After a few days, I realized that Nichols used these sessions to relax and engage the cast, especially its "high maintenance" stars. At the same time, these conversations also diverted and deflated any impulsive changes that the actors may have thought of outside of rehearsal. With this small-cast play, Nichols was building strong bonds of trust and collaboration in the cast, knowing that he had plenty of rehearsal time to direct it.

Although you should expect actors to take your direction and motivate it, you also need to be specific about what you want. Many directors believe giving notes and direction is an intellectual exercise in articulating the most effective, rational, and well-phrased notes, but that's only one method of communicating. You will spend your career learning how to elicit what you want from each actor, finding the "language" she will understand and respond to. One actor may respond to an unrelated story that is emotionally compelling and relates to the circumstances of the character. Another might respond to a detailed, specific note that calls upon his formal actor training. The director's role is a combination of jobs divided into many parts: leader, artist, psychologist, evangelist, coach, advocate, judge, and persistent trailblazer. Improving your communication with actors requires a basic understanding of the most popular approaches to acting and actor training.

Managing the rehearsal room also means effectively addressing any conflicts, and dealing with what I call "Rehearsal Killers," including:

- Actors who wait to commit to choices until audiences arrive. This behavior stalls everyone else's work, including yours. It also may reveal an actor whose process has become indulgent or disrespectful, assuming that everyone else should rise to her talent and expertise before she begins work. The only tactic that I have found useful with these actors is a combination of complimenting their talent and at the same time chiding them to help the company by being more engaged.

- Actors who mumble in rehearsals, making it difficult for others (and you) to hear and respond. Again, they hold back group progress. Tell them to speak up.

- Actors who paraphrase. Early in rehearsals, many actors struggle to learn their lines. This leads to occasional paraphrasing. If the paraphrasing extends into scene work and run-throughs, confront it immediately. Otherwise, other actors are not given their cues, the scenes wander, and the story loses momentum. Persistent paraphrasing may be a sign of actors who are not disciplined enough to learn the lines properly. When working on a new play, paraphrasing will drive the writer crazy. When working on a script with heightened language or verse, paraphrasing will drive you crazy.

- Actors who can't or won't learn their lines. Working with your stage manager, establish a time in rehearsal when you expect the lines to be learned (e.g., after blocking). If you have adequate rehearsal time, give the actors a series of rehearsals to call for lines. Later in the process, ask the stage management staff to assign someone to take "line notes," marking incorrect or omitted lines for each actor. And, of course, if the actor is playing a lead with an enormous volume of lines (e.g., Mother Courage or Hamlet), be patient. For actors who have severe trouble learning their lines, this problem may need careful and sensitive handling. If you see it recurring, discuss it immediately with your stage manager and mention it to the artistic director. If the performer is elderly or facing intense, unrelated personal stress, ask the stage manager to approach the actor first, discuss the problem and offer solutions. Are there mitigating circumstances? Does the actor need more rest? Stage management often schedules private sessions to help a performer learn lines, including reviewing lines just before scene work or a run-through. If line memorization improves, the problem corrects itself. The biggest warning sign of a more serious problem is when the actor forgets different lines in different scenes every day. This usually indicates a deeper problem with memorization.

- Actors who direct other performers. He says some version of the proverbial phrase, "is she going to do that?" or she turns to another actor, stating, "I need this from you in this moment." It doesn't matter if their comment is right or wrong, stop the practice immediately. And remind the room that all direction comes from you. This kind of behavior often reveals a self-absorbed or self-focused actor, worried more about his performance than his fellow actors or the show. These actors often blame everyone else but themselves when a moment or scene doesn't work. Direct them to the performance you want and hold them accountable

- Actors who resist (or don't want) direction. "I don't think my character would do that." These actors also spend precious time debating with the director or others why a piece of direction or design "won't work." However, this is very different from actors who are genuinely confused and asking for clarification on a piece of direction or blocking.

- Actors who are negative, angry, divisive, or defensive. This covers a whole host of behaviors that can stall rehearsals, sow discord or undermine the production and make your job much harder. This kind of behavior is often best handled by asking the stage manager to approach the actor first. If that doesn't work, meet with the actor and the stage manager. However, if the behavior continues, you must respectfully but firmly address it publicly. This adds to the importance of checking references during casting and hiring.

- Coaches and specialists who "direct" actors. When an actor complains that the voice/speech coach is giving direction or contradictory notes to her in private sessions, first check with the coach involved. Find out the other side of the story. This situation can be more complicated than it first appears. Individual actors may not want notes from a certain specialist, perhaps because they have a personal insecurity about that aspect of their acting. Some actors can be fiercely attached to a certain approach to voice, dialect, language, and text, believing that technical notes will make their acting less authentic. During my career, I have observed that actors in the US often respond best to notes based on psychology, intention, emotional response, and physical action. In the UK, actors often respond best to notes based on the voice, text, sound, operative words, and the progression of thought. Although I'm being overly simplistic, these practices emerge from the two cultures, which subtly reinforce norms of behavior, communication, and the expression of identity. The extraordinary voice teacher and coach, Cicely Berry, told me several times that she believed that more theatres should pair actors with directors from the other nation, such as a UK director matched with a US cast or vice versa. She was married to a gifted American sculptor and artist and refused to take sides, seeing the value of the two theatrical traditions. Returning to the situation at hand, you may also discover that one of your specialists (voice/speech, stage combat, choreography or movement) is indeed a frustrated director. As the director, you must decide specifically what needs to be done. Address the issue with both the coach and the actor involved. However, you can often avoid these situations by staying in daily contact with your coaches and specialists.

- Child actors who are being "directed" by their parents or an acting teacher. You can avoid many of these problems by ensuring that the casting director or coordinator speaks directly with parents and guardians at auditions about the practices and policies they must follow if their child is cast. At the first rehearsal, the stage manager should repeat these rules and expectations. Ask her to remind them that you are the sole director, and that **no** parent, guardian, or acting teacher should coach, give direction, or work on scenes with their child; this will only be done in rehearsals by you. In addition, neither the parents nor guardians should be allowed inside the rehearsal room, unless explicitly invited. Also, encourage any willing and capable adult actor in the cast to serve as a professional mentor for each child. Often the actors who play "parents, relatives, etc." will look after these young actors, but don't count on it. Indeed, when the actress playing Mrs. Cratchit or Peter Pan dislikes working with children, you might want to re-think hiring her for this role in the future. Often the best choice of a mentor is an actor who is a parent. Large theatres with more resources will hire a "child wrangler," who will help these young actors learn lines, complete homework, burn off extra energy, make entrances and exits, and navigate the "drop off" and the "pick up" by parents or guardians. Please don't misunderstand, I love working with young actors. It's refreshing and eye-opening, but I also know the value of keeping them concentrated on the work at hand. Remember to review their scenes frequently. When in doubt, lead the young actor step-by-step through his role. For dialect, line readings, and projection, begin this work immediately. Encourage the adult actors in their scenes to speak at "show" volume during scene work and rehearsals, because making a significant change in volume when moving into the theatre can prove daunting to the child actor.

- Working with celebrities and stars. Contrary to popular opinion, many actors who have become celebrities or stars are collaborative, creative, disciplined, eager for direction, and committed to the overall production. Their fame and success is justifiably based on their talent, artistry, and collaborative skills as an actor. Yes, the opposite can be true. Demanding, self-involved, and temperamental stars can wreak havoc on a production, and conflicts between two or three larger-than-life stars can create more drama offstage than onstage. Dealing with these actors is challenging but can also prove rewarding. Remember that celebrity actors often bring greater press coverage for the show and larger audiences. If you can massage the egos, manage the room, give thoughtful, specific direction (adjusted to each personality), provide frequent positive reinforcement, avoid taking sides, and gain the trust of each performer, you can create a remarkable show and establish important, future relationships. For some directors, these situations are especially thrilling. Jack O'Brien (former Artistic Director of The Old Globe in San Diego, and frequent Broadway and West End director) once told me that he "loves, loves, loves" directing big talents and big egos. He finds the rehearsal process intensely rewarding, given the electricity, the inherent high drama, the extraordinary level of talent, and the increased potential to create an exceptional show.

- Film or screen actors who haven't worked onstage for some time. Even more challenging is the well-known television/film actor who has no experience in live theatre. This situation often requires additional resources in training or coaching, but also calls upon the director to evaluate quickly the most critical gaps in the actor's skill set and then proactively to address those needs, adjusting the rehearsal schedule as required. These needs can include: coaching in articulation, volume, projection or dialect; helping the actor adapt to the size and scale of the theatre; suggesting specific approaches to the physical style or period of the show; helping the actor understand the live interaction between audience and actor; or ensuring the actor builds the necessary stamina for eight performances a week. Always working with respect, you should call upon any relevant experiences and techniques you used when directing self-trained actors, conservatory students, or young professionals.

For the director or director/choreographer of a musical, a considerable portion of early rehearsals must be devoted to learning music and dance numbers. I attend many of these rehearsals to hear the music being taught and watch the choreography being developed. At the same time, I schedule with the stage manager any pockets of available time with the principals and chorus members with speaking parts to complete table work. During the first few days, I sketch in the blocking with entrances and exits, working alongside the choreographer and music director, while recognizing that their work is of primary importance in these early rehearsals. Rather than working apart, directing alongside them saves time and develops a mutual understanding. With large musicals, additional time in early rehearsals will also be consumed by many fittings for costumes, wigs, and dance shoes.

Working with production staff

Chaired by the production manager, a **Production Meeting** is intended to give you and your stage manager progress reports on each design element (e.g., scenery, props, costumes, multimedia, sound). Production meetings can also include your designers, choreographer, music director, shop heads, fight director, and more. In many theatres, these meetings will include select staff from other departments, such as marketing, development, box office, and facilities. The production meeting gives you a terrific forum to provide an update on rehearsals (be positive!) and an opportunity to ask detailed questions or make specific requests, such as scheduling a time and date to test specially created items (e.g., the barber chair in *Sweeney Todd*) or especially challenging special effects (e.g., flying, live fire, or rain). The meetings also address questions, concerns, or problems in construction or preparation of any design element. If you learn that a specific department is behind schedule, find out the reason and its expected solution, but also take a moment to review with that department head the list of your priorities. For instance, having Laura's collection of glass animals in *The Glass Menagerie* is more important to the actors than having the "show" sofa for the living room. Production meetings also give you time to get to know the technical team leaders who will realize the production. It's important to express your appreciation to the assembled group at production meetings as this encourages each staff member to create the best possible production.

Walking the shops every week is a casual and effective way to find out the progress of each department, answer questions, and to meet individual staff members. The personal connection you make with a staff member working in the shops often pays off in tech and preview. Ask the stage manager to schedule appropriate times and days for you to walk the shops (outside of rehearsals).

During rehearsals, it's imperative that you stay in frequent contact with the creative team, especially your designers. You will want to engage them in solving any problems that emerge in rehearsal. They will be working with shop staffs to adjust or improve any elements as the pace of construction and rehearsal accelerates. Shop or department heads typically know to contact a designer about any changes or requests from rehearsal. If a designer is not timely in responding, contact her personally. If she doesn't respond quickly, step in and make the decision. However, do this only when it's urgent and necessary. In general, don't let the staff "go around the designer" by approaching you directly.

Scene work

After blocking the entire play, directors move on to scene work. These rehearsals typically begin with a review of the initial blocking. If the amount of time since blocking rehearsals is several days, this review often needs a lot of help from the stage manager, who has written down the initial blocking, which the actors may have forgotten. Having blocked the complete script, you will have learned much about the playing space and the best ways to use it. Use that accumulated knowledge to adjust the earlier staging as needed.

Scene work allows you to focus on the acting and the storytelling. You can question earlier choices you or the actor have made, solve key moments of interaction between characters, and fill in the details of each actor's part, including the character's gestures, the way he walks and talks, and so on. You can clarify motivations, operative words, the flow of thought and emotion, etc. When I become stuck, I often ask the actors to sit down with me and read the scene again a few times until we figure out what's happening. In storytelling, you can clarify and enhance the most important moments, score how the scene progresses, solve blocking problems, and work on stage composition. It's also a good time to observe how the actors listen and respond to each other.

Anne Bogart has a wise and useful quote about directing: "You cannot create results. You can only create conditions in which something might happen."[1] This is invaluable counsel. If you push for a particular performance, you short-circuit the actor's necessary process of discovery that's needed to create a fully realized character. You're avoiding the hard work of guiding each artist to create a three-dimensional character. It's important to remind yourself that **you** will not be performing on stage every night. Without the chance to develop a foundation, most actors cannot build a strong and reliable performance. Whenever I have directed a cast to jump to results, I have regretted it. This method creates a broad "sketch" of the show, but not a sustainable performance. Little can grow or improve, and the constant repetition of the same "results" leads actors to play for audience responses, rather than to enact the story. As an artistic director, I believe such directors are shirking both their responsibility and their artistry.

Once the actors are contracted, I reach out to each of the leads and begin conversations about how they view their character and my artistic vision of the play. This is especially helpful when an actor is playing a famous role, such as Cleopatra or Hamlet. In part, I want to help the actor avoid any conscious or unconscious pressure to create the "best" Hamlet or Cleopatra ever. Of course, that is impossible to do. More important, that relentless internal pressure can push the actor into excessive research about each word and line, or uncover every choice made for a scene in past productions. Such research can tempt an actor into deciding his interpretation and performance before rehearsals begin. An effective antidote is talking about your artistic vision for the play, throwing out several ideas for interpreting the character, and moving the actor back to his personal intuitive and emotional responses to the role.

During rehearsals, you as director must guide, persuade or force each actor towards your unified concept. If Tom in *The Glass Menagerie* wants to bring Tennessee Williams' late middle-aged rage and bitterness to the play, Laura wants to find a contemporary, feminist pluck and bravery to her role, and Amanda wants to be only caring and compassionate, then you must prod each of them back to your vision for the play.

During scene work, encourage the actors to try different approaches to scenes or moments. Use the rehearsals to add aspects of the character that layer in depth and nuance. Don't foreshadow the ending. When the actors have experienced the play's powerful and emotional ending, it's very hard for them to push aside that emotional knowledge. It is your job to help them do so. Return to the script and regularly remind yourself and the actor what the character knows and doesn't know when entering the scene, and what he then realizes, experiences or discovers by the end of the scene.

Scene work is also the best time to reinforce the working environment/ culture of the room. Make your expectations explicit. If other actors or understudies are in the room, is reading newspapers, checking smartphones, or resting permissible? Do you expect the company to focus on the work being done? What's an acceptable level of background chatter or noise? You can choose a collaborative, joyful, and engaged rehearsal room for a comedy or a quiet, attentive, goal-oriented, and serious room for a drama. Decide what is best for you, the show, and the company and then establish the boundaries.

If there are disagreements or conflicting ideas, you must decide what ideas to try or not, and then move on. If you encounter disruptive behavior or negative attitudes, deal with them in the moment. Much of this is taken care of by stating your expectations at the first rehearsal. State in advance how you expect actors to handle problems or complaints about another actor; I make it clear they should bring any significant concern to me privately. When they do, listen and respond. If you need time to think about the situation, state explicitly that you will consider it and decide what to do. Otherwise, your silence is often taken as tacit agreement. Once you've decided what to do, return to the actor and inform him of your decision and move on. All of these decisions should be based upon what works best for the show and your production.

An important note of caution! In the theatre, we hire actors to express strong emotions and find deep, personal connections to their roles. For the director, it's vital that you never assume that strong opinions and lively debates are automatically problematic or intentionally challenging your authority or another actor's choices. If you want an engaging, animated, and committed rehearsal room, you must create the safe place for strong opinions and heightened emotions. However, you must also learn to recognize when passionate and creative debate turns negative or destructive.

Every director needs cultural knowledge, continuous education, and help to work with artists from other communities, backgrounds, races, religions, life experiences, and traditions. Your sensitivity and awareness must be authentic and respectful. You can only build this level of communication by listening to and learning from members of each represented culture. In today's increasingly divided and intolerant world, every professional theatre director must publicly recognize and affirm the value of diverse artists and voices in our world, no matter the race, sexual orientation, religious practice, political belief, economic background, or cultural upbringing of the playwright or actor.

When directing a play that dramatizes intense conflicts and crises between different cultures, races, ages, or beliefs, encourage everyone representing each community to speak up. When directing a play includes such conflict or when a playwright uses archetypal roles in opposition to each other (e.g., anti-immigrant politicians versus undocumented Latina immigrants; Arab terrorists versus ultra-conservative Israeli nationalists), facilitate or ask for a facilitator to openly discuss what the play means to each actor (e.g., "why were you drawn to this play?"). Discuss what the writer hopes the play will reveal to artists and audiences. Each of us has some level of bias or distrust of others. We are easily tempted to blur the line between the role and the actor who is playing it. These discussions help to focus the rehearsals and performances on the importance of the play, and they often unify the company into achieving the best possible production. Stop any comments or conversations about what scene or moment the playwright should have written differently; lead the actors to fulfill the script as written.

After completing work on a scene, it's good practice to review it before moving on. If working sequentially, I often choose to review several scenes at the end of the day. Before moving on to full reviews of a multi-part show, I first schedule a review of each part. "Part" is a useful term and avoids confusion with the "Act." An older play may have three, four or five acts and I may want to combine them into two parts. After completing scene work for each larger part, we review it.

Preparing to move

As the studio rehearsals are proceeding, stay in daily contact with the production manager to ensure you have the latest production information. If you think it's needed, ask for a production meeting shortly before moving to the stage. It's the most direct and quickest way to find out what's coming or what's not ready for tech, and to address specific challenges and discuss possible solutions. When the load-in of the set is nearing completion, ask your stage manager to arrange a visit to the set, stage, and backstage areas. She will check with the production manager, technical director, and stage operations head to determine the best time for you to visit without interfering with the work onstage. Walking the set is the best way to collect information about, and solve problems with, the stage and scenery **before** the acting company appears for the first rehearsal onstage. With your stage manager, check the following:

- **Sightlines**. Will the performers and the action be visible to the entire audience as currently staged? Are there unexpected sightline problems? To complete your check, stand in the auditorium and ask someone to stand and move around the stage.

- **Places of heightened focus or power on the set**. We all know how powerful downstage center is, but are there other spots that have strong focus?
- **Actor/audience relationship**. Are there any visible challenges, such as a large gap between the stage and the front row? How far is the last row from the stage? Is the largest part of the audience above, below, or at the same level as the actor's faces?
- **Acoustics**. At what volume will the actors need to speak? Is the space conducive to the human voice? Are there aural dead spots or is the theatre plagued by echoes? Upon arriving to direct at a major resident theatre, the company manager who was driving me from the airport to housing casually mentioned that the worst place in the theatre for an actor to stand and be heard was downstage center! This was the result of a renovation several years earlier by a famous architect who spent millions on the lobbies, but little on the stage areas. It was common knowledge among the production staff, but no one had told me. This comment saved me many hours in the rehearsal room and in tech, although it proved challenging to convince several actors that downstage center was not a useful position.
- **Entrances and exits**. How will performers and crew navigate entrances and exits? Are the crossover spaces located where you anticipated? How long will it take an actor exiting on one side of the stage to enter on the other side?
- **Safety issues**. Check entrances and exits, stairs, doors, ramps, and the placement of lighting or sound equipment that affects entrances or exits. What's the access to backstage, dressing rooms, green room, etc.? Are there adequate handrails or grips to navigate the set?
- **Scene changes and special effects**. If there are complicated and/or important technical elements involving actors, transitions, and scene changes (traps, flying scenery, etc.), or special effects, ask the crew if they can demonstrate how each will operate prior to tech. This is very useful for learning timing and the operation of traps, crew-driven or automated scenery, etc. Many, many times during my career, these on-stage demonstrations have revealed significant differences between what I had been told and reality. In addition, these visits give crews extra time to address specific problems before tech.
- **Meet the stage crew!** Getting to know the backstage crews before the show moves into the theatre begins building your relationship with those who will be "running" the show every night in performance.

The stumble-through

As the name implies, this rehearsal is often an awkward first review of the entire play. Typically, it's a stop-and-start process, because the stage management or production crews will "change" the scenery and props for each scene. I manage expectations by setting it up as a time to review the play and see what we have. Success is making it through the show, while not attempting full-on "performance". For the actor, it's often a discovery of many things, including a reminder of the dramatic journey of her role, how much or little time she has between scenes, and the overall arc of the play.

For the director, it's a time of discovery about your staging of the play. Does each scene tell its action while moving the play forward? Is the arc of the script vivid and clear? What's the shape and condition of each actor's work on his role? Use the stumble-through to check your entrances and exits and identify traffic jams. Take specific notes, but also keep your focus on discovering which scenes, moments, and roles need the most attention. Use the stumble-through to create a roadmap for the remaining rehearsals in the studio. For a musical, it's an opportune time to hear the music, see the choreography, and watch the acting and the staging within the context of the entire show. This provides an excellent opportunity for you to discuss the progress of the show with the music director and choreographer and, if necessary, ask for revisions or alternative solutions.

First run-through

As the name implies, this is the first time to review the entire show at tempo, except for crucial scene changes which will be made by the stage management staff. First run-throughs are often attended by the artistic director who will take notes. Designers and department heads may attend to check their design choices against the physical actions of the actors. Wardrobe crews and stage crews who will be "working on the show" may visit to understand the action and timing of the scenes so that they can begin their paperwork.

Run-throughs are useful for both the director and the actors. Reviewing the entire play gives the actors a chance to integrate all the acting elements (acting, interpretation, dialect, blocking, and lines including changes or cuts), in the order in which they will follow in performance. For the director, run-throughs are invaluable opportunities to experience the play or musical again as a whole, watch the impact of the show, and determine what needs fixing. A run-through can also be an exhilarating moment for any production, as the entire company watches the individual and group performances, and the storytelling takes shape. Depending upon the rehearsal schedule, many actors will not have seen some scenes or moments for several days. As director, take specific notes for each actor as well as any general observations relating to the journey of the play. In addition, seize this moment to encourage everyone's work in moving together to achieve your vision.

"Designer Run-throughs" are pre-scheduled rehearsals for designers to see the current staging and, if needed, adjust their designs. The run informs their instructions to the various shops. Often these pre-scheduled run-throughs occur the day before the lighting, sound, and projection designers focus their instruments or finalize the installation of equipment in the theatre. Lighting designers often use a script with ground plans on the facing page to mark where the action takes place, while the composers and sound designers check that cues are correctly placed in the script and appropriate to the action. Backstage and wardrobe crews attend these rehearsals to check their own paperwork and charts regarding scenic changes, costume changes, special effects, and safety issues. Following a designer run-through, some theatres schedule a production meeting to share comments, questions, and concerns with you, the designers, and shop heads present. If there is no meeting, check in with each designer or shop head. For the director, it's important to give companywide notes and specific notes to each actor as soon as possible—either immediately following the run-through, by email, or at the beginning of the next rehearsal.

Orchestra/Band Rehearsals and the *Sitzprobe*

Most productions of musicals now involve the use of wireless microphones, multiple monitors, and sophisticated sound-mixing consoles. During the last few days in the studio, the music director begins rehearsing with the orchestra (or band) in a separate room. Both the music director and the conductor (often the principal keyboard player) will disappear from the room while they teach the music to the orchestra. Typically, another keyboard player or pianist is hired to cover these rehearsals. Part of the last few rehearsals in the studio is devoted to bringing the orchestra and the singers together for the first time. Borrowing a term from German opera, the *Sitzprobe* (literally translated as "seated rehearsal") gives the music director time to integrate the two groups—orchestra and singers—during a rehearsal. Although the instruments and voices are not "mixed" and balanced yet, it's an invigorating moment when the full sound of the orchestra meets the expressive singing voices of the actors.

The last day in the rehearsal studio should include a run-through, because the extended process of tech and dress rehearsals often delays the next run-through for several days. However, this is a judgment call on the director's part. Given the time and readiness of the show, you may need to fix or adjust moments or scenes, rather than schedule another run-through. Avoid the two extremes: (1) scheduling several run-throughs without holding proper notes sessions, or (2) working on moments and scenes obsessively but never running the show. The former repeats (and often "sets") the good and the bad in performances, while the latter deprives the company of much needed familiarity and confidence necessary for their performances and the production.

At the end of the last day, the stage manager will describe the process of moving to the theatre, when and where to meet the following day, any changes in hours or calls, and more. This is an excellent time for you to give a brief overview of the process you will be pursuing with the arrival of the design elements. Explain your expectations, including how everyone deals with any concerns or problems regarding any design element. Finally, I encourage every director to acknowledge this moment as a significant step for the production, and briefly remind everyone of what they've learned so far and what our goals are for the production. I thank everyone for their hard work and the progress made in the studio.

6

Moving to the Theatre through Final Dress

Leaving the rehearsal room and moving to the theatre is a rite of passage for any production, one which brings heightened excitement for directors, actors, stage managers, and crews. If you've done your job well, the run-throughs will have improved and built confidence in the cast. The show may well have become as strong as possible—in the studio. Another sign that you're ready to leave the room is a falloff in responses, because those watching have seen the show repeatedly. It's time for the stage.

The real joy in moving **out** of the rehearsal room and **into** the theatre is the introduction of a three-dimensional working set, backstage, and audience area which replaces the taped-out studio floor. It's a heady time when the work of the designers, shops, crew members, and actors comes together for the first time. For the director, moving to the theatre is your opportunity to collaborate and lead designers, craftspeople, crew, and technicians to realize your directorial vision and to deliver the most exciting and engaging production possible. Rehearsals lengthen, with longer hours allocated for tech and dress before previews, and post-rehearsal production meetings begin.

Practices and expectations

Theatres differ in their schedules and practices from the first rehearsal onstage through opening night. Prior to moving to the theatre, find out the theatre's practices and express your own preferences for tech and dress to the production manager and your stage manager. Ask the artistic director about her expectations for previews. For the first paying audience, every theatre expects a presentable performance, but what does that mean to her? Does the theatre consider the First Preview a "performance that's 90 percent finished" or a "work in progress"? This will inform your planning through final dress.

Theatres typically follow a similar series of steps in mounting a show in the theatre: spacing rehearsals, technical/dress rehearsals, preview rehearsals and performances, and rehearsal on opening day. However, these steps may be impacted by the schedule and resources of the theatre. For instance, your spacing, technical and dress rehearsals may all be compressed into a couple of days. As mentioned in the previous chapter, consider the total time you have for "spacing rehearsals." This will determine what you need to accomplish before tech/dress begins. You may have time to work through the entire show, or you may need to devote time to reviewing scenes with complicated staging, such as physically active crowd scenes, fights or musical dance numbers.

First day in the theatre

When everyone has gathered in the house, I begin the first rehearsal onstage by asking the crews, designers, and shop staff members to introduce themselves. Shop staffs and backstage crews rarely receive enough recognition. I lead a round of applause for their past work (the set) and their future help, and then discuss my intentions and focus for the day. I remind actors and crew members how any concerns or problems they might have with any design or technical element should be addressed.

The stage manager and I then discuss the schedule of the day, and let the cast know if any designers or technicians will be working concurrently during our "spacing." For example, lighting and/or projection designers often work "on top" of the spacing rehearsal onstage. They are checking their design, plot, and focus of instruments with the set and the acting areas, and experimenting with different combinations of color, intensity, timing, and sequencing. Primarily, they are building (or continuing to build) basic "looks" for each scene in the play, recording a series of cues and moving forward. This work significantly speeds up the process of tech, and gives the designers more time to refine and improve their designs before opening. However, the lighting designer is frequently working on a different scene than the one being "spaced." Remember to direct the actors to perform the blocking **as rehearsed**—in other words, don't adjust blocking to "find the light." Assure the actors that these lighting issues will be fixed during tech. Professional designers are very good at not disrupting the rehearsal, but give explicit directions to the cast what to do if there's an unexpected blackout, etc.

Then I turn the rehearsal over to the stage manager. This is a symbolic and practical ritual. He sits at the center of communications with the many professionals who will run the show, including backstage and wardrobe crews, and technicians operating light boards, traps, scenery, and equipment. He's in direct contact with the designers, shops staffs, and more. Although I will be heavily involved with every aspect of the show, the stage manager is the person who will manage the show and create the template for its best execution. Stage managers cover several important topics, including:

- Safety First and Emergency Policies, including procedures for exiting the theatre in case of fire or dealing with a medical emergency.
- Sign-in sheets, access to dressing rooms, collection of valuables, restricted areas, etc.
- After pointing out any features of the set that require special attention from the actors, she invites the actors to walk the set, check the entrances and exits, crossover areas, location of cue lights, lighting or sound gear in the wings, and backstage areas, including dressing rooms, wardrobe, stage operations areas, and the green room.

Testing your staging

Hopefully, you've been given time for a "Spacing Rehearsal." As the name implies, this is time to review your current blocking and see how it works on the set before the arrival of full tech. The stage management staff will have measured and marked with bits of colored tape where they believe the furniture or props are placed, based upon measurements from the studio. You should adjust the placement of furniture and props as needed.

For the director, it's an invaluable time to evaluate the physics and kinesthetic realities of the set. Determine how the set can best serve and support the necessary physical action of the play. Change or adapt your blocking and staging to the realities of the stage, the set, and the house (i.e., the audience seating area). Spacing rehearsals give actors time to familiarize themselves with the playing space. I help the actors find solutions to blocking problems, but also encourage the entire company to work with the stage manager and crew to begin solving timing of entrances and exits, requesting cue lights or glow tape, and finding the best offstage location of props. I focus on the flow and progression of the staging and the clarity and effectiveness of the dramatic storytelling. At the same time, I check the vocal and physical energy and the physical size of the acting needed in this theatre. Encourage the actors to sit in the seats at the back of the house, on the sides, and in the balcony to watch and listen. Don't spend time on scene transitions or technical elements; solve those issues in upcoming technical rehearsals.

If you have an assistant, assign him specific tasks, such as checking sightlines from different seats in the house whenever you make a blocking change onstage. Ask him to write down notes and questions on playing spaces, blocking, acting, and scenic or design elements. When working with an assistant, I ask him to follow me closely with the script and a notepad in hand. Given my tendency to move around the theatre constantly during spacing rehearsals and to forget where I set down my coffee cup, script, notepad, or cellphone, he helps me not waste time trying to find the script and notepad. More important, he helps me prioritize my requests for revisions or adjustments in scenic elements and any needed re-blocking or scene work.

Technical/dress rehearsals

The director's primary responsibility during these rehearsals is to integrate all design and technical elements with the acting, the staging, and the dramatic storytelling of the play. At the same time, a director must evaluate how each design and technical element supports, and hopefully enhances, her artistic vision for the production, and how well the designs work together.

Tech/dress is the time to refine, revise, and possibly change any design or tech elements that need improvement or that don't work.

This is a particularly enjoyable and fascinating stage of rehearsal for me, because I can collaborate with and lead the design team. Watching their designs appear and evolve is very exciting, and our conversations are often insightful and inspiring, as I discover each designer's talents, aesthetics, and learn their opinions, tastes, and personal perspectives on the play. Just as you persuaded the actors, stage managers, and production assistants to band together in the studio to reach a higher artistic vision, you now have the same opportunity to motivate the designers, technicians, and crew members to enhance your artistic vision and create the best possible production.

Unless the show has very simple design elements and technical needs, you need to turn your focus away from the acting and storytelling and turn it towards the design elements and the stagecraft needed to mount the performance. This means the bulk of your time will be spent with the designers and shops heads, the stage manager, and the crews running the show. You will be helping actors solve specific problems or concerns, but these are related to the design/production elements being teched.

During tech rehearsals, a director will have a myriad of tasks and problems to solve. You will be working with: (1) the designers and shop heads to incorporate their designs; (2) the technicians and backstage crews to learn their tasks during the show; (3) the actors to figure out the best use of the costumes, props, sound cues, traps, flying scenery, special effects and more; and (4) the stage manager to manage the entire process, including the calling and cuing while staying in constant communication with everyone involved.

At the first tech rehearsal, every design or tech element should be "show" ready—that is, fully finished and ready to go. This includes props (e.g., chairs, tables, letters, swords, stage blood, tea sets or beer bottles [and the liquid used], edible food, electronic cigarettes, live fire torches or machetes, rifles or pistols). The scenery should be finished, painted and prepared for tech, including all elevators, traps, escape stairs, doors, moving platforms, special effects, rigs for flying, or crossovers, etc. And sets of costumes and accessories (e.g., wigs, facial hair, prosthetics, fans, canes, hats, umbrellas, etc.) should have been placed in dressing rooms for each actor. The lighting and/or projection designs are prepped and ready to rehearse. For a play, sound designs and music cues are ready to play; for a musical, the sound designs include wireless or wired mikes for actors and orchestra, monitors for the actors, speakers for the audience, and live mixing consoles for a musical.

Tech rehearsals often include additional hours, such as a "10 out of 12" which refers to two 5-hour rehearsal sessions within a 12-hour window.

Having an organized, smart and effective stage manager is invaluable for any director during tech/dress. Hopefully, she has had the time and support to meet with the designers outside of rehearsals to talk through the show and write down specific cues. From the studio rehearsals, she already knows and understands most of your preferences in calling cues (i.e., on which line, reaction or physical beat), but she will need considerable time during the tech/dress rehearsal to write down the numerous cues and notes from lighting, sound, projections, scenery transitions, actor entrances, traps, flying elements, wardrobe, special effects and more into her stage manager's "bible," the show script she will use to call the show in performance.

Theatres follow union rules in allocating time inside the rehearsal hours for the actors to dress (usually 30 minutes). Often it takes longer! This is not surprising, since it's the first time all the actors have dressed in their full costume—from shoes to wigs. Once everyone is dressed for the top of the show, I gather everyone in the house so they can see each other's costumes, and share a few moments of mutual admiration. I thank and applaud the designers, shop staffs (often present), and the crews, and then explain the day, and what we hope to accomplish (e.g., tech through the end of Act 1). Again, I remind actors and crews how I expect any disagreement or problem with a design element to be handled—namely, through myself or the stage manager. I hand the rehearsal over to the stage manager.

The stage manager has made sure every crew member understands their tasks and journey through the show, and has spoken with the relevant actors. She calls everyone to places, and we begin teching through the show, from "house lights to half" through the final "blackout." The stage manager runs the rehearsal from her command center while the director leads the process. We work through every scene and transition in order, but stop to revise or fix whatever needs attention; repeat it, and then move on. Given the technological advances in theatre lighting, sound, monitors, keyboard and consoles, the SM's bible can contain hundreds of cues for lighting, sound, projection, automated scenery, musical pickups, traps, actor warnings, and entrance cues.

Tech will and should always be a deliberate process, working on each transition, lighting state, sound adjustment, or prop that actors or crews use. Don't expect the rehearsal to resemble a stumble-through. It's a stop-and-go process. When something doesn't work, the stage manager will stop the rehearsal, and you and the relevant designers, crew members, and actors will try to fix it. If it's fixed, the moment will be repeated and you'll move forward. If the moment cannot be fixed at the time, the team will brainstorm solutions to try in the next rehearsal.

The crew will need time to learn and rehearse the transitions, including traps, flying objects, and special effects. I encourage the crews and the actors to stop if they encounter any significant problem onstage (e.g., a trap won't open, a prop breaks, a set piece gets jammed in its floor track, or shoes are too slick for the choreography). With the appropriate designer or shop head, we talk with the actor, and see if the problem can be resolved quickly. Otherwise, we note it for revision before the next rehearsal and move on. In advance of scenes with highly physical activity, such as a large dance number, I stop before the scene starts and turn over the rehearsal to the choreographer to review the activity in costumes with show props. After the review, we run the scene and move on.

For special effects or risky tech moments involving any actor, we will stop the rehearsal and review the action. I verify that the actor is dressed in the correct and complete costume. If the actor is falling into a trap, being hung or shot, or undertaking an especially tricky stunt, we take time for the crew to explain the mechanism to the actor. Then I ask the technical director or a shop member to demonstrate the mechanism (they likely built it and have been testing it since before tech). Then the actor uses it and practices with the crew until she is comfortable with the action.

Decide in advance with your stage manager and wardrobe head how to handle costume changes. Experienced wardrobe staffs will have detailed charts of all changes, which include each actor's first costume, the next one, the dresser(s) assisting her, the change's location, and timing. Individual information is posted for each actor in the dressing rooms and the various changing areas offstage, and every dresser will carry a copy of the chart. For a large musical, this spreadsheet can be enormous and complicated. Often more is going on offstage than onstage when many actors are making full costume changes at the same time.

If the clothing is elaborately designed or the show has transitions where many actors are changing in a brief period of time, you may want to rehearse some changes first and then run them in sequence. My preference is to let the actors and crew try the change during the rehearsal. If the change isn't completed in time, we (the designer, wardrobe staff, and actor) stop and discuss solutions (often it's practicing the change several times). If the problem persists, I ask the designer, costume shop, wardrobe staff to solve it in a fitting with the actor as soon as possible.

Putting on a costume for the first time is often a thrilling but disorienting moment for the actor. The clothes, the beard, the hat, the boots, and all will affect his physical presence and emotional state. Actors will forget lines, miss entrances, look stunned or worried, as they seek to integrate these most intimate and personal elements into their performance. By the next rehearsal, they will have adjusted to their costume and begun exploring how to use it to best advantage.

The director and the stage manager must lead the tech rehearsal to keep the process productive and moving forward. When any element is repeatedly stalling the process, identify what it is and figure out a solution. Adopt an alternative plan, if you must. If the lighting designers and their board operators are taking excessive amounts of time to build each cue, setting timing and sequencing, and make revisions, then the tech rehearsals become laborious and enervating to all. Check your observations with the stage manager, but immediately talk to the designer and ask him to pick up his pace. If he cannot, ask him to prepare outside of rehearsal. Lighting designers may be overly deliberate or slow for several reasons: some build lighting layer by layer and spend a lot of time trying out different looks; more commonly lighting designers are not fully prepared, because they've accepted too many design jobs in too short a period of time or they may be dealing with a serious crisis outside of rehearsal. Without rancor or disrespect, let him know your expectations. Move forward with the other areas of the show. Make a mental note to add some questions to your future reference checks of lighting designers: Are they well-prepared for first tech? How do they respond to direction and how fast can they make changes?

Keep in constant contact with your stage manager, because she is running the rehearsal, and incorporating revisions or changes. At the same time, she will be sending actors for fittings or special sessions. There are always pauses in tech when the stage manager, the lighting, sound, music, and projections designers are re-writing a cue or fixing a drop or piece of scenery. Use these pauses to give notes to the actors onstage or simply chat with them.

Working with designers

Responses to the creative choices of the designers in tech and dress vary widely among directors. At the beginning of the first tech/dress rehearsals, I respond only to the most immediate or urgent problems, such as re-cuing the top of the show or working out the use of a trap. Otherwise,

I like to spend some time watching the designs in action onstage. After watching several scenes, I can better articulate my thoughts about all the designs.

During tech/dress, I talk with the designers frequently about specific ideas or notes, but I also use this time to figure out their tastes, working styles, and preferences. I appreciate direct conversation and even debate with each designer about what's important to each of us and what's best for the show. It's helpful to build a relationship with your designers before the start of tech/dress. Of course, that's easier when you have worked with a designer. If you haven't, get to know the designer as early as possible. At the director/designer conference, if I am visiting a designer's home city, or when a designer is visiting the theatre to check on the build of the show, I invite him to have a meal, coffee and tea, or a drink. Although we discuss the show, we often spend time talking about our upcoming projects, who we both know in the field, and so on. It's a brief but helpful way to get to know each other.

In my opinion, discussing any costume reveals many differences in personal style and taste among actors, designer, and director. This can be trickier than the other elements, because actors are wearing the designs; many actors have very strong opinions about what clothing, colors, and fashions they believe works best for their physique, or how well the clothes "inform" their character. For the director, first dress is a time to listen to actors, take notes, but also to support publicly the designer's work and artistic vision. Conflicts are largely avoided if you spent time during rehearsals in fittings with leading actors or have visited the costume shop with the designer to see the work in progress. Such visits begin a continuous conversation with the costume designer, that helps you to resolve any problem between the actor and the designer.

If you believe a design element doesn't work, figure out why. What's amiss? If it continues to distress you, speak to the designer, but also mention your concerns to the production manager. Is the issue an inconsistency within one designer's work? Or is it a larger problem—are one or more designs pushing the production in the wrong direction? In my directing career, the majority of design and technical problems originated with one design or design element. For me, it has happened in two ways: (1) the designer (and/or I) lacked personal knowledge of the location or time period of the play, and (2) the style and tone of the play or musical is off-base or wrong. For example, if you're directing an iconic American play which is set in the American South, the director and the designers must dive deeply into the clothing and customs of the specific community in that moment and that time. Otherwise, the costumes (and the behaviors and dialects) can range loosely from New Orleans to Charleston, a distance of five states and 800 miles. As a geographic reference point, Vienna, Madrid, Oslo and Venice are approximately the same distance from London. In the second circumstance, I attended a director/design conference for a comedy by Molière and described my concept and directorial approach, which was followed by an animated conversation about the revelations of human foibles exposed by this painful and brilliant satire. When I received the preliminary costume and scenic designs, I was startled by their style—broadly comic, eye-blindingly colored, and verging on cartoon. This approach shocked me, because I knew that a visual world that competes for comic effect with the acting usually forces the actors to perform the play as a broad farce. Such imbalance must be addressed the moment it happens.

If it's a more serious problem with design or tech that you believe undermines or damages the show or your artistic vision, immediately talk to the designer and notify the production manager. Few theatres have the human resources to make large changes, but you may be able to find a suitable compromise. Whatever you decide to change, always talk with the actors and the crew before any change arrives onstage.

Never let one designer dominate the creative team. Talk with each designer regularly, in private and in public. Give notes, ask for suggestions when needed, and make timely decisions. You alone decide what works best for the production. In the absence of a strong director, creative team members may try to fill the void. The choreographer starts telling the lighting designer how to light his dance numbers, the costume designer will make choices that look gorgeous but don't support the character's actions in the script, or the scene designer will ignore the serious safety concerns of the fight director. You are the director. Handle these problems and decisions professionally and efficiently. Not surprisingly, these stressful situations lead many directors to work regularly with the same, small group of designers.

Take care of the actors

With difficult or long tech rehearsals, make sure that you or the stage manager keep the actors informed of what's happening during a gap (e.g., working on lights, resetting the traps, writing cues). During these pauses in action, re-engage with the actors. If voices are tiring, suggest they speak at medium volume. If fatigue is setting in, ask them to "mark" their performance—go through the actions, language, and intentions but not at full bore. Remind them that tech/dress is a great time to review lines, scenes, explore the set, work with props, and anticipate any upcoming issues with blocking or physical action. A wise stage manager will ask each actor to remain backstage after every exit or scene transition in case it needs to be repeated. This saves enormous time. Often the stage management staff will incorporate final fittings or adjustments for costume, wig, shoes, weapons, or props into these rehearsals. If the play requires one or two herculean performances, such as Salieri in *Amadeus*, Phaedre, or Johnny "Rooster" Byron in *Jerusalem*, make sure you take care of your leads during the long hours of tech.

Dry Tech and Cue-to-Cue Tech

Theatres sometimes utilize a concurrent process with your last few days in the rehearsal studio, termed "Dry Tech." Without the performers present, stage managers work through the show with lighting, sound, projection, and scenic designers to set and record cues in the SM "bible." This method is often used when tech/dress time is short, such as stock, repertory, or outdoor festival theatres.

Depending upon the time and resources available for tech/dress, theatres may follow a "Cue-to-Cue" tech rehearsal. As it sounds, the rehearsal proceeds by working through every cue in the SM "bible," including lighting, sound, scenery transition, special effects and more, until it's acceptable, then jumps forward to the next cue. The two practices present a challenge for the directors, actors, and crews. Not only do they not review each scene for acting and lines, but it's also very difficult to determine the length of time between cues and to learn the arc of the show.

The temptations of tech

A common trap for a director is taking too much time in tech/dress. This happens for several reasons. If the director and designers (and not just lighting designers) work and re-work each transition, scene or moment repeatedly before moving on, the rehearsal becomes agonizingly slow and enervating. Although a quest for perfection is laudable, it must be balanced with the time allotted for tech/dress and the needs of the entire company. A studied and overly precise approach to tech can deprive the company of having a run-through before the first audience. This practice became so problematic that AEA now has a work rule, mandating at least one run-through before the actors face a public audience. In addition, directors and designers who become obsessed with each cue often discover that the show in performance demands a different kind of design, cuing, sequencing, and forward motion. However, by this time in rehearsals or previews, it may be too late to make changes.

Another example of taking too long in tech/dress occurs when tech is used as an overly collaborative, trial-and-error process. This leads to trying out many ideas, but often settling for a workable but lackluster solution that appeals to the most people in the company. One of the weaknesses of the collaborative/trial-and-error model is never fixing specific problems via a consistent and compelling style of theatrical storytelling.

Another trap is rushing through tech/dress without addressing the individual moments or problems in the show. Some directors leave those to the designers, the stage manager, and the actors, which is unwise. Most successful and experienced directors use tech in a way that combines the two approaches: the first is an obsessive dedication to excellence for select moments and scenes of dramatic importance, and the second is an iterative process of doing and revising, then doing and revising again.

Another dangerous temptation for a director and design team is spending a lot of time and resources preserving a "conceptual" idea or design element beyond its useful life or merit. An advocate of mine, the late John Hirsch, was directing a production of *A Midsummer Night's Dream* at Canada's Stratford Festival during his tenure as artistic director. He and his designers (led by the remarkable Desmond Healey) created a prologue that included the four major plot lines (i.e., the Court, the Lovers, the Fairies, and the Mechanicals) but primarily focused on alternating battles between Hippolyta/Titania and Theseus/Oberon (both conflicts are mentioned later in the play). Following a long-used casting tradition, two actors doubled in the four roles. With dazzling direction reinforced by spectacular design elements, the prologue was visually stunning, but lasted eleven minutes. As previews approached, shorter, tighter versions were tried, but with unsatisfactory results. Hirsch listened to his collaborators, his actors, and the preview audiences, and then cut the entire prologue before opening.

Although the prologue was very expensive, Hirsch told me (a young assistant director on another show) that the most important lesson I could learn is how much time it absorbed in tech and dress. Although he had believed his prologue was necessary to introduce his directorial vision, he "cut" his losses before the first preview. All of us will make these mistakes, which in hindsight appear obvious. Each of us can easily become too enamored or fixated on our conceptual ideas and be blind to their true value and significance to audiences.

Once you have completed incorporating all the technical and design elements into the show, you will begin running the show in dress rehearsals. The detailed and deliberate work of tech/dress has taken your attention away from the acting and the running of the entire show. Although the dress rehearsals allow you (and your design team) to see the entire show at tempo, they also "return" it to the actors. You will be making additional tweaks and improvements to the technical elements, but now is the time to bring your attention back to the actors. In addition, no matter how tight your rehearsal schedule is, it is vital to schedule time for a dress run without stopping **before** the first audience. This requires you to re-balance the needs of tech with the needs of the acting.

Final dress rehearsal

One of the revered superstitions of theatre is the thought that "a terrible final preview presages a great opening." In today's theatre, I think I would rephrase it: "a terrible final dress presages a great first preview." Although it's magical thinking, it can be true, because the rehearsal prior to final dress is demanding with long hours of work in tech and dress. In addition, we may have reached the limit of what we can do before an audience joins us. Rather than obsessing about detailed notes and changes, I remind myself that final dress allows me to examine the bones of the production. Is it a well-built engine? Is it on track? Are the actors finding their pace and energy in the show? Is it beginning to stir my emotions and thoughts again—resembling the first reading? If this proves true through final dress and into previews, it means the show will endure, improve, and grow.

7

Previews through Opening

The **First Preview** is another rite of passage for every production. The experience can be invigorating, surprising, and wonderfully affirming. Or terribly disappointing. Ready or not, you're in performance and showing your work to a group of outsiders—the audience. Over the next few performances, they will let you know what works and what doesn't. It's a good time to remind yourself and the company that the preview audience is not a "judge" but rather a final and invaluable collaborator. No script turns into "theatre" without an audience. Yet there's no avoiding the anxiety that a first audience brings. Before the first preview, the best direction to the company is often: "Do the show as we've rehearsed it, enjoy yourselves when you can, and we'll talk afterwards about what we've learned."

Although the first preview brings the first paying audience, many subsidized and commercial theatres also use previews to build word-of-mouth and attract price-sensitive subscribers and groups; as a result they are often filled with older adults and long-time patrons. The vocal responses can be more muted, but these audiences often bring more concentration, discernment, and appreciation to the show. In fact, preview audiences can be the best audiences, because they are happy to be there and respond genuinely. Marketing directors also use the previews to start building their audience for the run, drawing on a wide spectrum of the community in age, demographics, backgrounds, etc. They know from experience that no single demographic can deliver the necessary sales in today's world.

During the performance, consciously try to relieve your anxiety by shifting your attention to the staging, the acting, and the audience response. Ask your assistant to take your notes, so that you can keep your eyes focused on the stage. Listen, watch, and learn from what the audiences tell you about the show. Note the moments or scenes that are surprising, revelatory, or especially effective in the storytelling and the staging. At the first preview, the audience often reminds you of the many compelling moments and scenes that you admired when you first read the play aloud and that have been forgotten during rehearsals. Many theatres schedule only a limited number of previews. To take advantage of two or three previews, you must concentrate on the overall arc of the storytelling, and the scenes, moments, transitions, or events that most need your attention. I find preview audiences remarkably helpful, because they force one to zoom back and see the show anew. Watch for the following:

- Note the moment when the audience fully engages in the performance, otherwise known as "suspension of disbelief." I use the phrase, "when the other shoe drops." Although the audience has been listening to the show from the first line, this is the moment they give themselves over to the experience and forget they are watching a performance. If the moment is consistent across a couple of previews, point it out to the company. Tightening cues and increasing pace in the earlier scenes will often strengthen the moment's impact.
- Note any moment, scene or transition when the audience disengages or grows restless. Also, are there sections of the play that evoke odd or inappropriate reactions?
- When the audience doesn't respond to key plot points or significant events, determine why. Can the audience hear the actors? Have you clearly directed the audience's focus to the moment? Have you set up the progression of the scene to build to this moment? Is the pace of the show too fast for the audience to follow or is it too slow to keep their interest? Are the actors bringing the necessary urgency to the scene?
- Is a piece of tech ineffective, clumsy, or taking too much time? This can be a sound or light cue, a scene change or special effect. Is the show not gaining speed due to overly elaborate design elements or simply a lack

of time for the crew to rehearse? For example, long or awkward transitions can kill a performance's cumulative impact. They create a gap in the action, let the audience disengage, and force the actors in the next scene to re-catch the audience's attention.

- Observe the actors' performances carefully. In the heightened energy of a first preview, actors can rush moments, talk over audience reactions, push too hard or pull back, making their work more intimate by lowering their volume. Experienced professional actors sense when this happens and will make automatic adjustments in the next performance. However, you will need to help the less experienced actors. Give the entire company specific examples and check their awareness of what happened. Other issues you may need to address in acting include:

  - After crafting a nuanced performance with an actor, did he revert to "bad habits" or follow impulses that distorted or undermined the scene (no matter how much the audience enjoyed it)? If so, give notes and correct this behavior immediately.

  - Is the size of an actor's performances too big or too small?

  - Are the actors connecting, listening, and building scenes together?

  - In a comedy, you and the actors are inevitably reminded that not every moment will (or should) get a laugh. When you've created a merry rehearsal room, often you and the actors are tempted to add physical bits or tweak line readings for more laughs. Work to eliminate any unnecessary bits or embellishments.

  - In a tragedy or drama, is the audience "getting ahead" of the story? In other words, have you directed the actors to play the end of the show **before** the ending? This can have a deleterious effect, and the show becomes labored when it should be tumbling forward ever faster to the shattering moment of climax, recognition, and tragic resolution.

  - Do the actors earn the ending? Have they taken each major step in the journey? You may need to remind them of the play's journey or re-calibrate performances or your direction. Is the actor weeping or sighing so much that the audience doesn't? If so, you need to direct them to internalize the emotions so that the audience will respond more fully. This recalibration of a performance can be difficult, but it's worth the effort.

  - Previews can also inform or change your opinion about an individual actor's performance. Sometimes audiences will contradict your opinion of an actor's work, especially if you became fixated on his shortcomings. If you perceive the audience has a much different reaction, give positive notes to the criticized performer. In the worst cases, you may discover that you've ignored other actors in those scenes. Asking any actor to make significant changes to his performance after weeks of creating and pursuing his character without direction is unsettling and frustrating. Approach the actor with care, confidence, and optimism, but ask for the specific changes you want. And explain why.

After each preview, immediately go backstage and check in with the actors. It's important to thank them, compliment their progress, and mention any overall thoughts you may have, as well as listen to what surprised, encouraged, or concerned them.

Work rules based upon the relevant union agreements affect whether or not you can hold a post-performance notes session. The time you use during post-show notes is often subtracted from the next day's rehearsal. Calling post-performance note sessions is a judgment call by the director. Many actors prefer to hear the notes after the show, so that they have time to think about each note and begin to integrate it into their performance. On the other hand, you may need time to review your notes and think about solutions first. Or is it more important to give the actors your overall observations of the preview, group notes, and a list of what you will work on the following day? Many directors now use email to send notes to the actor, especially for smaller, detailed notes. This substantially reduces time in a notes session. As director, you will need to decide what works best for you, and be aware that it may change with each project—you will feel much more confident to give notes after a 90-minute show than a three-and-a-half-hour one.

Post-show production meetings

Previews are usually followed by production meetings, which are chaired by the production manager. These meetings include all designers, crew heads, the stage manager, and you. For musicals, add the music director, choreographer, conductor, sound designer and, at times, the musician's union representative or contractor. You and the stage manager give notes for revisions, changes or re-thinking any design element, scene transitions, etc., followed by a discussion of possible solutions. The production manager will then ask each designer and department head for any additional notes and requests and conclude the meeting by scheduling the next day's work up to and between the hours of rehearsal and preview. Pay attention to the various work calls, in case you want to attend one (e.g., to see new projection cues). Work with your stage manager to create a prioritized work list for the next day's rehearsal including time for the stage manager and crews to improve transitions or special effects, hold costume or prop fittings, revise stage fights, schedule sessions with voice coaches or movement specialists, etc. For a musical, allow time for music and dance rehearsals. During previews your most important work is with the actors. Now is the time to put the actors, the acting, and the storytelling front and center.

Invited Final Dress Rehearsals

Several theatres have started using the final dress rehearsal to invite people who otherwise cannot afford to attend: members of the specific communities that are represented onstage (e.g., members of the deaf communities for Nina Raines' *Tribes*); ushers and volunteers; and/or staff members and their families. However, final dress is now increasingly used as a marketing or development tool more than a community service. Marketing departments add group or club leaders, concierges from surrounding hotels, and media sponsors; and development departments add donors, government officials, foundation staff, in-kind contributors, and VIPs. If the theatre has scheduled an "invited dress" around a marketing or development "event," find out what it means for your show. Will the tech tables remain in the house for stage manager, designers, and you? Is it truly a working rehearsal? Can you or the stage manager stop the show or performance for an unforeseen issue or to fix a significant problem? How many will be attending? Who are they?

To set expectations, I like to welcome this audience to the "final dress rehearsal," and let them know the evening is a "working rehearsal." We may stop, fix a cue and restart the show, which will give them an insider's view of "live theatre in action." After covering the usual pre-show announcements, I thank them for attending, because their responses will help us improve the show prior to opening.

With cast and crew, I approach an "invited dress" as if it were the first preview. The audience may not be paying for a ticket, but they remain the first audience. For most actors, "invited dress" brings the same excitement and stress as a first preview. At its best, an invited dress gives the actors more confidence in their work and takes the pressure off facing a paying audience the next evening. However, you should be aware that these audiences often react more passionately than the paying audiences who will attend the next few performances.

Notes with the artistic director or producer

Artistic directors and producers often attend dress rehearsals and previews. Plan to schedule time to meet with them and get their notes. If it's the next day, ask if they have any "high level" or "major" design or production notes that need immediate attention at the post-show production meeting. If you have serious concerns about any design element that needs revising or re-building, bring those issues up as well.

Most artistic directors will have attended the first read-through and seen a run-through and/or a dress rehearsal. They are naturally eager to see how the show has progressed and how the audience is responding. Of course, they also want and need the show to attract audiences and be of the highest quality possible. If the artistic director is out-of-town or directing another show, proactively stay in touch. Talk, email, or text with him a couple of times each week about the show's progress and do the same in person with his artistic and production staff. As we discussed earlier, artistic directors have very different working styles and approaches to notes. Some are blunt and demanding, while others are collaborative and positive. You may receive pages of notes or just four or five observations. When I directed for an acclaimed actress turned artistic director, she told me that her notes were intended to "stir things up and to startle the director into better choices." She delivered her notes and opinions dramatically and didn't allow for conversation. Unfortunately, she didn't tell me her philosophy until the second time I directed at her theatre. For the first, I had not followed my own practice of getting to know the artistic leader before previews. In truth, many artistic directors are very supportive, giving notes and perspective that help you improve the show.

If an artistic director believes the show is in good shape in previews, he is, of course. relieved. He will give you notes, tell you what he likes or doesn't like, and push you to make the production better. If he is worried or concerned about the condition of the show, he will be more demanding and specific. No matter the circumstances, bring your script, a notepad and pen, and an open mind to note sessions with the professional who hired you. Listen to the feedback and write it down, unless you have already taken the same note. If you have taken it, say so. Ask for clarification when you don't understand a note or observation. Few expect you to incorporate every note, but they absolutely expect you to listen to and consider each note carefully, try out their ideas, and incorporate their most important ones. If the artistic director wants a significant change, incorporate it during the next rehearsal or convince them otherwise on the spot. Think about each note in the context of the specific performance that the artistic director saw, your directorial vision and the audience response.

Of course, the notes may or may not be helpful. Broad or general notes such as the proverbial "faster and funnier" rarely help (unless it's true), but observations and suggestions regarding storytelling, the arc of a specific actor's journey, and the overall experience of the performance can be extremely useful. At best, an artistic director serves as an invaluable "third eye." Don't be afraid to solicit his advice for specific problems that you have repeatedly tried to solve. If it's a specific note to an actor, he can often suggest other ways to say it, or different approaches to the actor based upon his past experience. **Never** pretend to agree to a note when you don't. This is both disingenuous and unprofessional. You must show respect for the producer and have the courage to discuss your differences. If an artistic director asks for huge changes that you believe would be truly destructive, consider your options. As hard as it is, avoid becoming defensive. Instead, take a moment to reconsider the note and evaluate how it might improve or damage the production. If you disagree with the note, begin a conversation to ascertain the reasoning and purpose behind the note. Discuss your own ideas and intentions. If you cannot persuade him, strive to come to an agreement about the next steps. Only in very extreme cases should you consider leaving the production. Despite the circumstances, you don't want to disrupt or undermine the show or your company, you need the full fee (the final portion is paid on opening), and you don't want to damage your reputation (i.e., becoming known as a "difficult" director).

Time becomes more precious the closer you get to opening. Many aspects of the production may need attention and time to revise and improve. This can include tightening cues, integrating new or revised props and costumes, reviewing new or revised lighting, sound, music or projection cues, and scenic elements that have been purpose built or re-engineered. Working with your stage managers, rigorously focus the rehearsal time on: (1) the acting and the actors, (2) the technical needs, and (3) your directorial vision of the show. If a note can be given outside of rehearsal to the designers or production staff, do so. Prioritize your list and work with your stage manager to decide the most efficient way to run the rehearsals, which may also include costume fittings, coaching sessions, among other things.

With the actors, work on the scenes or portions of scenes that require the most attention. Make time to integrate any new design element that directly affects any actor, such as new costumes, props or pieces of scenery (e.g. weapons, glassware, furniture, doors, traps that have been re-engineered, etc.) Establish a hard-and-fast rule that **no** significant (new or revised) prop or costume or scenic element touched or used by an actor ever appears onstage without rehearsal. Any change must be shown to the actor first. When it's a minor change, the actor makes the decision to use it or not. When in doubt, rehearse it. At each break during rehearsal, review the work list with your stage manager to prioritize what's most important to accomplish in the time remaining.

Begin notes with the positives, not with what didn't work and needs improving. Discuss the progression of the various sections of the play; illuminate how the play ebbs and flows, when they need to pick up the pace to build to a peak, or give themselves more time to absorb what's happened or been said to them. Describe the impact the show has on you and on the audience in performance. Avoid general praise or criticism, such as "I love your work in that scene; it's very exciting," or "You don't seem fully committed in Act 2, pay more attention to that." These are meaningless and are of no help to the actor. Instead be specific about "why" you admire that scene. Specify the notable moment within the actor's journey. State "why" a moment is not working for you. However, when praising an actor, resist pointing out a specific line reading or facial expression. This is directing for a "result" and it can make many a professional actor self-conscious about the moment in future performances. Celebrate any surprising or extraordinary discoveries or moments that lifted the show.

This is the time to give detailed and specific notes to the actors, and **rehearse those notes.** For companywide notes, you can give general notes for larger scenes, crowd reactions concerning pacing, focus, or audibility, but always include specific examples of the change you want, and **rehearse the note.** Don't avoid giving public notes to any actor, no matter how important she is (or thinks she is) and **rehearse the note.** After the group session, I also give private notes to some actors, when more explanation or conversation is needed. Private notes are also an excellent time to have conversations with your leads. It's especially helpful when redirecting an actor's journey through the part. And, yes, **rehearse the note**, if the actor requests it. In addition, I also rotate the practice of giving private notes through the entire company to check in with each actor and focus my attention (however briefly) on him.

Major changes in previews

If you feel the show would benefit from a major change, consider asking for it, if there is time and the theatre has the resources. If you believe a major design element needs extensive revisions or even replacing (e.g., a new costume for a leading role, re-engineering of effects or scenery, or a radically different approach to lighting), first discuss the change with the relevant designer. Hopefully, you've had a prior conversation about this change and they will be prepared to make it happen. As soon as possible, meet with your stage manager, the production manager, the designer, and artistic director (if present). Articulate why you want the change and how it will improve the show. If you've built a positive relationship with your stage manager and the production manager, they can provide invaluable help ennabling this change. At most theatres, the production manager has been given authority to support a director's or designer's request for changes up to a certain amount in labor and material costs. If your request exceeds that limit, the artistic director and/or managing director must approve it. This may delay the decision until the following morning. If the change is possible, confirm when it will arrive and be ready to rehearse. Let the actors who are affected know your plans and engage the company in accomplishing the change.

Bringing the ship into port

In my experience, the most challenging part of any show is the last 10–15 percent of the director's work. In the nautical world, the term "bringing the ship into port" was in use during the time of large sailing ships; it referred to the hazardous steps of getting the ship dockside. As the captains knew, considerable nautical skills and talent were required to bring a ship within range of the channel or harbor, navigate it through a web of natural or manmade hazards (including other vessels) and "berth" it. In the theatre, I use the term to acknowledge the rewarding but risky practice of transforming a solid production into an excellent one. If successful, this practice can create the conditions for extraordinary theatre; if unsuccessful, it can damage the show. This work takes skill, craft, and artistry that can only be learned by directing many, many shows. Some never learn this practice, either discounting its importance or understandably not wanting to risk upending the production before opening. To master it, the director must use the previews to "zoom back" and see the show anew. You must let go of the many details that have naturally obsessed you during tech and dress and look at the show holistically. The presence of audiences often helps me identify how the show works, what its cumulative effect is, and what or who might be holding the show back and not letting the performance take flight. The director must rigorously question himself about what would make the show great.

- Do the reactions and overall experience of initial audiences match your original vision and expectations? At intermission, I spend time in the lobby listening to audience members' conversation for any repeated comments or observations. If a trusted friend or colleague attends a preview, I don't prep them in advance, but follow-up after the performance, asking about the actors, the impact and clarity of the story, and their overall experience. I encourage candor in their comments.
- Is an individual actor's performance (especially in a leading role) received with the same enthusiasm and excitement that you felt in rehearsal? If not, why? What can you do to rethink and redirect the actor's approach in major moments or in the role?
- Are there any conceptual ideas in staging, design, or acting that add little or nothing to the production, even though you deeply treasure them? A quote commonly credited to William Faulkner (though also to Oscar Wilde, Alan Ginsberg, and others) is "In writing, you must kill your darlings." This phrase applies equally to a director and asks you to consider cutting your most favorite moments or conceptual devices. Do these beloved creations advance the story or are they precious, self-indulgent, or unnecessary?

None of these questions is intended to confuse a director, and it's true that we often lack the time to consider them. However, they can be very useful to review when you feel a production is not rising to its potential in performance. Once you identify a significant weakness or problem, take a moment to review the time and resources you have left. Also, is the weakness in your control to change? If not, let it go. When you have very limited rehearsal time before the opening, you may decide wisely not to go ahead. However, if you do, consider what the show will gain and what it might lose with the change? Use the creative team, your assistant, the stage manager, and (perhaps) the artistic director as sounding boards. Does the idea excite, engage, and inspire them? If the problem lies with an actor's interpretation or performance, evaluate her capacity and willingness to change course this late in the process. Any last-minute major change demands a couple of things from a director: a specific plan of action and a brilliant and persuasive speech that acknowledges the prior hard work, articulates the need for the changes, and most of all highlights the remarkable potential for a much better show. Then stay true to your decision and make the change.

Hopefully, such a major change is not needed. And you can use your final rehearsals in previews to work on specific moments or transitions that will help the actors, crews, and the play move forward. As you move closer to opening, focus and reduce your notes to those that are most important. If you've given an actor an interpretative note more than three times, let it go. Only rehearse when absolutely necessary. Keep in mind that giving a large volume of notes, making changes in blocking, or the rearrangement of scenes during previews often results in inconsistent performances, as actors seek to incorporate your notes and changes on the fly during previews. Give the actors the freedom and confidence to find the tempo and flow of the show. However, these last few rehearsals are also excellent opportunities to talk to the company about your original artistic vision, inspiration, and hopes for the show. Remind them (and yourself) of the larger purposes and ideas behind this production, while acknowledging everyone's hard work in achieving the experience. After the long hours of tech, dress, and previews, this reminder often invigorates and inspires the company, because it reminds them of their original excitement about the show.

It's a rare actor who can seamlessly incorporate changes on opening night. Short of disaster, forgo giving significant notes or changes for a couple of performances before opening night. It's often a good time to review scenes or moments that unexpectedly went awry the night before, but otherwise keep the last rehearsal casual and upbeat.

Opening night

There are wide-ranging expectations and traditions within the professional theatre field regarding opening night, based on the past practices at the theatre, the different sectors of the field, and the size and scale of the operation (i.e., Broadway musicals versus a small ensemble's devised work). Common practices include gifts, cards or notes, flowers, memorabilia from the show, backstage speeches, and celebrations after opening. Ask the theatre's staff about their opening night customs and what might be expected of you. The tradition of rousing, emotional, and inspiring backstage speeches by producers, artistic directors, composers, playwrights, and/or professional directors is inconsistently practiced across the field.

Opening nights can be wonderful. Some are brilliant, joyous, and triumphant. The energy between performers and audiences is electrifying and sustained. There is a palpable feeling that the evening was an astonishing experience for all. Other openings can be odd. Although the show is in terrific shape, the performance can easily become slightly strained, off-balance, or askew. This can be due to many factors. Despite confidence in and approval of their performance in previews, many actors feel the pressure of opening night. Many want to get through opening night and begin the run. Often the opening night audience includes spouses and partners, close friends or relatives of actors, agents and managers, industry leaders, local theatre professionals, press and critics, Board members, donors, and VIPs. This audience is frequently not the most attentive, encouraging, or enthusiastic group. Often these audiences seem harder to "impress." Pre-show cocktail receptions can mute the reactions of trustees, donors, and VIPs. Some of these special guests are present due to their public or corporate responsibilities, not their love of theatre. Local theatre artists can also dampen the evening, by being silently critical (unresponsive) to the leading or guest actors but cheering their friend with an enthusiasm above the size of the role. If a lot of complimentary tickets were issued for the opening, there can be large gaps in the auditorium—the ever-present danger of free tickets. Keep in mind that we (theatre professionals) are acutely aware of these differences in performance, but most audiences are not.

Watching an opening night can turn any director into a nervous wreck. For years I watched the first act of any show (even one that had received tremendous response in previews), noted every directorial mistake that I had made, and then frantically berated myself for choosing the wrong profession. After talking with staff and patrons at intermission, I would calm down for the second act. This level of anxiety leads some directors to pace at the back of the theatre, hang out at the lobby bar, or avoid attending the show altogether. This can happen to the best of us, too. Ingmar Bergman, one of the twentieth century's most influential and acclaimed film directors (*The*

Seventh Seal, Smiles of a Summer Night, Wild Strawberries, Cries and Whispers, Scenes from a Marriage) frequently worked in the theatre. He directed more than 170 productions at leading theatres all over Europe. In interviews and writings, he shared that opening nights brought him panic, anger, sadness, and frustration, and often ended with his becoming ill. Although extreme, I believe Bergman's reactions at opening nights reveals two common, psychological issues for a director: we're giving up control (we're helpless—there's no more rehearsal!) and we are feeling the beginnings of "postpartum" sadness at leaving this company. It may be opening night for the actors, but it's closing night for the director. My own feelings of anxiety only began to subside after our son had his first few piano recitals. Watching this gifted pianist, who happened to be our son, play in recitals with much older children, I worried he was not prepared to compete, but then realized that there was "nothing I could do" if anything went wrong. I could not control or even affect the outcome. My presence and my attention was the most useful thing I could bring to the recital. That's good advice for any director on opening night—be present and attentive.

After the performance, immediately run backstage to congratulate and thank the cast and crew personally. For the rest of the night, follow these suggestions:

- Never, never, never, never give critical notes on opening night. Smile and congratulate each performer, crew member, etc. If you're furious or disappointed at someone's performance, grin and bear it. All of us who work in the theatre are exhausted, excited, relieved, but very vulnerable after the opening of any show. Each of us can be deeply wounded by a harsh comment or criticism.
- Thank the artistic director for hiring you. Thank the managing director, the production manager, and staff members for their work on the show.
- Celebrate!

When directing a professional production, your contract is complete after the opening performance. If you live out-of-town, you will be leaving shortly. In my career, the scheduling became so tight that occasionally I had to leave one city in the early morning hours after opening to begin rehearsal of another show in another city that afternoon. But before you leave town, arrange time to meet with your stage manager, who is responsible for keeping the show in shape or "as directed." Although she has watched and listened closely to your direction in the rehearsal room, she's also been consumed with running tech, calling the entire show, staying on top of changes, and improving her own timing. Stage managers appreciate your taking the time to discuss with them any concerns you have about the production, such as what scenes you think are most likely to wander off course or which actor might be tempted to "improve" his performance in the wrong way. Many stage managers will ask for advice on tempo, notes that they didn't hear when you spoke to individual actors, or methods for handling specific performers. According to union rulebooks, actors are contractually required to perform their roles "as directed." However, every audience changes the show and every actor discovers new moments in performance with their fellow cast members. That's the beauty of live performance. Instead of rigidly restricting the stage manager to what happened on opening night, a director should talk with the stage manager about the shape and intent of the production. The best stage managers will know your vision and have considerable experience in judging the merit of any new acting moment or innovation. They have a firm hand on the show, and will communicate well with actors and crew, and communicate with you if there's a significant change undertaken or being proposed by an actor that is questionable.

After the show has opened, keep in touch with the company and the stage manager. Read the performance reports when you receive them. Stage managers write up reports (often based on a form created by the theatre) that include information on each performance, including time the show started, length of show, general observations for the acting company, requests for repairs, additional supplies or edibles, audience size and response, any unusual incidents (e.g., audience member having a medical emergency), and notes for tech staff, etc. Because they are widely distributed throughout the organization, stage managers keep them brief and to the point, then follow up in detail with individuals and departments. They provide you with a useful snapshot of the show. Follow up with the stage manager with any questions or concerns.

Tell the theatre if you want sales reports, press, and/or reviews. If you are thick-skinned, you can check the responses and comments online. Stay in touch with the artistic director after the show closes. Build your contacts and network. Add the emails, postal addresses, telephone numbers, and social media addresses of each company member you enjoyed working with. Sign up for the theatre's media announcements that include announcements of future seasons.

Part III

Advancing Your Career

8

Finding Your Next Directing Job(s)

The length of time between your first professional production and the next one is unpredictable, even when your show receives good reviews, positive audience reaction, and generates strong ticket sales. During rehearsals, when you're reasonably confident that your production will be a good representation of your work, invite your mentors, colleagues, and friends to see the show, but also invite a short list of strategically chosen professionals outside your network with whom you want to share your directing. Better yet, have your agent or manager send the invitations to that shortlist. Your near-term goal is simple: you want to be hired at more theatres.

If your production receives bad reviews and generates poor ticket sales, take a couple days to recover and then think about what went wrong. However, make sure you don't show your upset or frustration to the cast and company. Jot down your observations in your journal. Put down any part of your direction that didn't work and figure out what you need to improve in your directing. After an unsuccessful show, we often need the help of a trusted colleague or friend to "see" how the performance doesn't work. With a troubled show, accept the responsibility for any mistakes as the director, but also recognize that failure most often is the result of a collection of missteps or mistakes in many areas of the production, such as the casting, the acting, the design elements, technical direction, stage operations, or the script. Be realistic in your self-criticism and determine if any of the problems were **not** in your control as the director. Also, find out what the artistic director thought of the show. He likely can identify what was wrong with the direction apart from what was wrong elsewhere. Keep your head up and look for another show at another theatre.

When you've directed a strong production, your best and most immediate advocate is the artistic director or producer. Next are the staff of the producer's office or theatre, and the professional artists with whom you have you worked. During rehearsals, take time to meet and talk to the managing director and the executive leaders. Executive or managing directors and production managers talk frequently with their colleagues from across the country, and also meet at theatre conferences and industry events (including negotiations of collective bargaining agreements). Senior staff members often move to other theatres. The point is that positive word-of-mouth spreads rapidly in our field and often leads to more work.

The value of recommendations by a producer or artistic director underscores the importance of not "burning bridges" when directing a show. The theatre field is notoriously small and intertwined, reducing the "six degrees of separation" to two or three. Asking and pushing for the best possible production is necessary and commendable, but demanding that the theatre meet your artistic vision beyond its promised human or financial resources is ill-advised or risky if you want to work there again. That approach often reveals more about your personality than your artistic brilliance. Certainly, it demonstrates a lack of understanding, respect, or consideration for the theatre company. Condescension, outbursts of anger, verbal or emotional abuse, picking on individual performers, or taking out your frustrations on shop staffs and backstage crews will undermine your future employment. Artistic directors will not want to hire you back, and this sort of behavior can threaten your prospects if you want to lead a theatre in the future. Yes, there are brilliant and highly successful directors who are exceptions to the rule. They may be prone to sudden outbursts, erratic behavior, unreasonable demands, and lacerating notes. Behavior like this creates a rehearsal atmosphere of fear and dread, as everyone avoids becoming the next target. Mark Clements (Artistic Director of Milwaukee Repertory Theatre and Derby Playhouse, with directing credits at the Chichester Festival, Roundabout Theatre, Hampstead Theatre and many other European theatres) says:

A [freelance] director can't get away with that kind of behavior today. For the first couple of generations of directors and founding artistic directors, the theatre field sought and supported one artist's singular vision, no matter how anyone else was treated. Today's world won't allow that, and most artistic directors won't tolerate destructive or abusive behavior. It can damage the show, not to mention the staff and company.

This does not mean that directors cannot be demanding in their direction; but today you are also expected to create a productive, collaborative, fulfilling, and positive environment that brings out the best work in everyone.

Finding agents and advocates

If you don't have an agent yet, find out who represents the theatre directors you admire and/or those who work frequently. Although some agencies list their directing clients on their website, many do not. The fastest way to find out is to ask your colleagues, mentors, and fellow directors who represents them. Once you have a list, make a habit of inviting these agents to your shows. If you have an especially close relationship with another director or artist, ask if he will refer you to his agent or agency. When you're invited to meet with the agent, take your resumé and be prepared to give a brief bio and overview of your goals and interests as a director, as well as a list of writers, composers, theatres, and producers you hope to work with. After the meeting, jot down your personal and professional reactions: Did you personally connect to this agent? You don't have to become friends, but do you think you'd enjoy working with her? Does she understand your artistic aspirations and career goals? Does she bring expertise and skills that you need? Can she advance your career?

When you're offered representation, ask what that means. Many agents verbally agree to represent you, but want to "see how the relationship works out." The next level of commitment is a verbal offer to represent you. The most significant commitment is a legally binding signed contract. This means you will be legally and financially committed to this agent for any directing jobs for the length of the contract. Consider both the agent and the agency. Find out how the agent and agency has worked with other early or emerging directors. Was it a positive experience? Does the agency value emerging directors like you, or do they focus in large part on their prominent or more experienced directors? Does the agent have sufficient power and prominence within the agency to advance your interests? An agent at a smaller firm often provides new clients with more care and attention; on the other hand, the smaller agency may not have the same access or leverage within the industry.

When you first secure representation, take personal responsibility to create a strong working relationship with your agent, and don't expect the agent to find you additional work immediately. Although it's frustrating to pay 10 percent of your fee when you personally secured a job, keep in mind that the agent and agency provides you with other benefits such as increased professional credibility and exposure; introductions to other theatres, producers, and professionals; and expertise and experience in contract negotiations and disputes. They also may represent other clients with whom you want to work. Increasingly, as in the movie world, the larger, more successful agencies put together "packages" for productions or projects that employ several of their clients. Stay proactive in finding your own jobs, and remember that the more you work, the more your agent will work for you.

Finding **Advocates** is valuable for any freelance director. These are not mentors; rather, they are experienced and influential field leaders, funders, colleagues, and media writers who have become fans. They can advocate for you in the field and provide personal recommendations and introductions to others. The strongest advocates can also provide useful advice, insight, and help. Two influential advocates in my career have been Ben Cameron (former executive director of TCG [Theatre Communications Group], the national service organization for not-for-profit theatres in the US, and program director for the arts at The Doris Duke Foundation) and the late Gordon Davidson (acclaimed artistic director of The Mark Taper Forum and then its parent organization, the Center Theatre Group, in Los Angeles). When I served as Board president of TCG, I developed a close working relationship with both of these men. Although I never directed for Gordon, he and Ben gave me stellar recommendations to the Denver Center, which vaulted me onto the interview shortlist. That process ended with my being hired as producing artistic director.

Next steps

As you direct more widely, you should aspire to direct at a higher level in the profession. To succeed, you will need to build your resumé, create additional relationships, and enhance your reputation. Each of these tasks takes considerable time, care, and effort. The theatre is a person-to-person service industry deeply dependent on personal relationships. Achieving greater artistic and financial success as a director depends upon whom you know, the relationships you forge and nurture, as well as how well you stay connected. As you increase your network of producers, playwrights, actors, designers, theatre writers, etc., keep in touch through social media apps, texts, emails, meetings, drinks or coffee, or telephone calls. There is an art to "keeping in touch" that should consciously adjust to each person in your network of contacts. How does each prefer to receive information, how often, and how much? Find out and use each person's preferred method. Avoid "blast" emails and postal mailings. Don't oversell yourself, because a thoughtful soft-sell approach is more effective than aggressive self-promotion. For instance, I dislike receiving large packets of information, photos, etc., that include a page of "glowing" quotes from critics, rendered in giant type sizes. Keep your resumé and your packet of background information to a few pages by including only what's relevant to the theatre. Keep your cover letter/email brief and to the point. Also, you don't need to send another resumé with any updates on your work, unless there are major additions or revisions. In addition, don't expect a response. Once my directing career took off, I became irritated and indignant by the lack of response from artistic directors of theatres where I had directed several times. When I became an artistic director, I realized why they hadn't responded. Artistic directors and producers receive enormous volumes of calls, messages, texts, emails, and postal mailings every day. They often don't have time to review everything, much less respond. However, a wise practice is to keep in touch with the artistic, literary, and production leaders you know, because they meet regularly with the artistic director. At all times, evaluate the true strength and depth of your relationship with any artistic director or producer. If you don't have a relationship, resist the temptation to keep contacting him frequently. If you haven't had a response in two or three years, stop bugging him.

Keep in touch regularly with your mentors and advocates. If they see your shows, ask for their frank observations. If they give you feedback, take note. Given their importance and connections in the field, they often possess the power to open doors for you, recommend you for jobs, and advance your career. If it turns out that your mentors and advocates don't have that kind of influence or won't use it for you, find new ones.

Communications and networking

Given the ubiquitous use of social media apps and platforms today, it's essential that a freelance director creates and nurtures an online presence. Personal websites for designers are commonplace and they are extremely valuable for displaying their portfolio of work, resumé, and contact information. Much of their work can be communicated by visuals. For directors, it's a trickier question, because visuals do not reveal much about our work. The advantage of a website is having a specific online place where you can post your bio, resumé, photos of productions, current and upcoming projects, news and reviews, and other related activities (such as teaching, serving on theatre panels, or receiving awards and grants). The disadvantage of having a website is the time, labor and cost required to create your site, maintain it, enhance it (e.g., optimization for search engines), all the while keeping your information up-to-date. As a director, think about the purpose your website will serve, who will be accessing it, and what you will post on it. Many directors find a website more useful once their careers begin to accelerate. As they gain wider recognition for their directing, the site attracts growing interest from the field about their recent, current, and upcoming projects. In the end, having a website is a personal decision.

Increasingly, social media apps are providing easier and less-costly ways of sharing professional and personal updates, information, contacts, and regular communications. Options increase every day and currently include personal blogs, collective websites devoted to a specific group of artists or directors (e.g., female, Latinx or Hispanic artists, actors with disabilities, etc.), and, of course, there are the dominant apps such as LinkedIn, Facebook, Twitter, YouTube, and Instagram. Experts in social media advise professionals to learn what each site or service is best used for, then define what you want from each site, based on your personal communication and networking needs. This includes defining what you want to share online. Which site do you pick to share private photos, messages and personal information with family members or close friends? Is it the same site you use to stay connected to the professional theatre field? Which site gives you the best opportunity to follow the artists, agents, directors, and producers whom you admire or need to know? On which service will you express your opinions and passions about political, cultural, social, and economic issues? Given today's severe political polarization and chaos, I believe it's both unavoidable and irresponsible for any artist to stay silent. But what's the best platform? How much time and energy can you devote to social media? How much time and energy **should** you devote to social media? Follow the rule that parents tell their children: don't post anything publicly or privately that you wouldn't want the entire world to see.

As you search for your next engagement, you will face a familiar barrier— one that every director encounters at times in their careers. The producer will state, "I need to see your work first." This is true. Artistic directors are very reluctant to hire you without having seen a production that you have directed. However, we also constantly check who is being hired by our close network of artistic directors, producers, theatres, and colleagues. We refer the names of exciting, new directors to each other. Often, we will take a chance on a new director when needing a replacement. My first two professional directing jobs occurred when a colleague recommended me as a replacement. In the first, the director withdrew from the show for a much more lucrative gig and recommended me as his replacement. Although the show was already fully designed and cast, I jumped at the offer. My second job arrived when playwright Romulus Linney (whose plays I had directed in workshops and readings) recommended me to a frantic artistic director who had lost her original director. Although I did not select the creative team, I did cast the show and loved the experience. Both of these "replacement" jobs led to additional ones.

Two other circumstances often lead to more work at additional theatres. In the first, you direct a "signature production." When you've directed an unusually successful show at one professional theatre, you may be asked to repeat the production (based on the same concept) at another. The second involves "co-productions" shared by a group of theatres. In a "co-production," you are contracted to direct a show shared by two or more theatres. For the first theatre, you direct with a full rehearsal period. Upon closing, the physical production is shipped to the next theatre, and you "re-mount" the show with the same cast in a much shorter rehearsal and tech schedule. The move and re-mount process may continue for months, depending upon the number of partners. The co-production model was intended to increase the human and financial resources for the entire production while reducing each theatre's share of costs. The practice of repeating the same production/concept or directing a co-production is an excellent way to direct at multiple theatres in different locations, work with several artistic directors, and establish relationships with staffs. In addition to building your resumé, co-productions can prove lucrative, depending upon the relevant union agreement. Many contracts require theatres to pay the full directing fee and benefits, regardless of the shorter length of time spent re-mounting the show.

As a director becomes more known, she may be "typed" by her significant prior successes (e.g., "she's very good with new plays by women" or "classic musicals"). If this happens to you, congratulations. You'll have more work. However, this "typecasting" may not align with your artistic passions, or you simply may want to expand your repertoire as a director. Whatever the reason, identify the titles, genres, types, or theatrical forms that you want to pursue. If you've become known as an exciting and effective director of new plays, do you also want to direct American musicals or European classics? Although you've been labeled as a director "good with physical comedy," is your true passion to direct plays by Euripides, Sarah Kane, or Arthur Miller? If you've become accomplished at creating immersive and interactive theatrical experiences in non-traditional spaces, do you yearn to direct at a mainstream theatre with more resources and staff?

Once you make a specific choice, take the time to consider if you need additional training or expertise. If so, find it and do it. Then tell your agent, mentors and advocates, professional colleagues and friends, and the artistic leaders that hired you previously of your new interest. Work proactively: If an established rep or regional theatre won't hire you to direct a Shakespeare play, find a stock theatre, a summer festival or respected conservatory program that will. Look for any opportunities that help you fulfill your passion first, then pursue similar productions at larger theatres. If you want to direct large-scale, commercial productions of musicals, pursue assistant directing for a Broadway or West End director. Such an experience will increase your working knowledge, connections, and relationships in the musical theatre. The past decade has created a new category of commercial directing jobs, namely the "resident director" or "associate director." Broadway and West End musicals often hire an associate or resident director who assists during rehearsals and previews, then attends the production regularly, gives notes and rehearses scenes to maintain the director's original vision and keeps the performance at high quality. In addition, they may rehearse understudies and replacements. On national tours, these directors travel with the company. These positions are union jobs, with appropriate fees and benefits, and will improve your techniques, skills, and expertise.

Knowing the field

It's vital that you stay informed about current trends in the field, keep up with the latest news, and know who's working where. Nowadays this is much easier to do, thanks to the internet. Theatre service organizations, unions, advocacy groups, media organizations, and trade publications are now online, and there is also a vast amount of information on social media. Select the ones that match your interests and your wallet. In the US, two prominent subscription publications cover the professional theatre. The *Theatrical Index* is a weekly, comprehensive listing (including producers and investors, general managers, theatres, composer/lyricist/writer, directors, cast, etc.) of current Broadway productions and their national tour schedules. It also includes shows in development, upcoming scheduled productions, and selected world premieres at regional theatres. *American Theatre* covers the not-for-profit field, with frequent postings, articles, news of leadership changes, annual season announcements (often listing the directors), results of fieldwide fiscal surveys and industry conditions, and monthly schedules of productions across the US and more. Of course, there are many free or low-cost websites, covering the field, including Broadway.com, Theatremania. com, the League of Chicago Theatres, and many more. If you want to find coverage of Fringe or Off-Broadway and Off-Off-Broadway shows, turn to *The Village Voice* or *Time Out* (New York and London). In the UK, *The Stage* provides comprehensive coverage of professional theatre. The UK Theatre Blog provides frequent updates. In addition to the theatre reviews, columns, and news covered by the major newspapers in the UK, there are other online sources with reviews and tickets sales via UK Theatre's online magazine, Exeuntmagazine.com, and the British Theatre Guide.

After a few years, many professional directors will have established their careers and will receive regular job offers from mid-sized to large regional or subsidized theatres. Working regularly for several theatres over time is gratifying, sustaining, and also helps you learn and mature as a director. The regional or rep directing fees can be competitive with those paid in New York or London, except for the Broadway, the West End, and the largest subsidized companies (e.g., RSC, the Royal National, Lincoln Center, and Roundabout Theatre). With a strong base of subscribers and single-ticket buyers, connections into the local community, and substantial contributed income (or in the case of the UK, government subsidy through the local Arts Councils), the larger regional theatres may have the resources to fully realize your artistic vision. If you're fortunate to direct several productions each year, you will need to develop the necessary organizational skills, capacity, and commitment to work on many productions at the same time, and the discipline to plan in advance for each show.

However, every freelance directing career is unpredictable (and far from linear). One season may bring multiple offers while the next may bring none. Or you may be offered multiple productions each year, but the timing doesn't work. For example, you receive four offers for the fall, but can only direct one, because of the overlapping dates. To make a living wage in either country, you likely need five or six productions a year. Each gig requires 3–8 weeks onsite, but the average is 4–5 weeks. When you add in the prep work, design meetings, casting, etc., you are easily spending two months on each production. If you do the math, 6 shows x 2 months = 12 months. From my experience, directing six shows in one calendar year is very rare and frankly exhausting. Unless you are making significantly higher fees, you will face economic challenges. Most of us need to find some way to supplement our income.

As a result, many directors pursue artistic staff jobs at professional theatres, with such titles as Associate Artistic Director, Artistic Producer, Resident Director, or Artistic Associate. There are many inherent benefits to these positions, including having an artistic home, having regular opportunities to direct shows, engagement with the artistic and management staffs, a reliable source of income, and perhaps healthcare and retirement benefits. The position of associate artistic director (AAD) typically pays the best, being a full-time position that works closely with the artistic director. This position often provides an opportunity to connect with the audiences and communities that the theatre serves, and represent the theatre at conferences and gatherings. If you plan to become an artistic director or producer, the AAD job gives you an invaluable, inside view of an artistic director's life. You will intimately observe effective and ineffective methods of artistic leadership and achievement.

In my opinion, working as associate artistic director can be the best job in the professional theatre and also the worst. The AAD may direct regularly, help select seasons, oversee certain productions, cast shows, or head major initiatives, such as new play programs. All of this depends upon the artistic director and the specific job duties and responsibilities she assigns to you. Some artistic directors resist delegating or sharing responsibilities with anyone else, while others want frequent collaboration. An AD's professional working style can range from controlling all decisions to collaborative partnerships. Also, artistic directors vary in their philosophy and practice in leading an institution. At one end of this spectrum are committed institution builders, and at the other visionaries dedicated to their own artistry. Some are interested in serving the artists and audiences at the theatre; some are interested in advancing their careers or changing the field. Each leans towards one end of the spectrum or the other, but most combine parts of each style of leadership into their own unique approach. In truth, the theatre needs both kinds of artistic leaders. The danger of the externally focused leader is that you, as the associate, may end up virtually running the artistic side of the theatre while waiting constantly for approval from your absent boss, who is directing elsewhere. The danger with the internally focused artistic director is having a boss who micromanages and/or is resistant to any new ideas. If you want to become an associate artistic director, do your research, find out the artistic director's working style, artistic vision, and openness. Review the job posting or description carefully to check for specific duties and responsibilities. If you are replacing someone, contact him for his experiences. In interviews or conversation with the artistic director, be straightforward, ask questions, and express your hopes for the job (based upon the job description). It's also very important for you to see the theatre's work in performance, with a follow-up conversation with the artistic director to compare candid perceptions about the show. In this way, you can determine whether your artistic sensibilities and observations align or not. If they don't, reconsider your interest.

Artistic producer or artistic coordinator is becoming a more common position in mid-size to large organizations. As the title implies, this is a "producing" position within the artistic staff, often charged with keeping each show or project's communications, tasks, and decisions moving forward within the larger organization. Depending upon the artistic director and the organization, this may or may not include directing and higher levels of artistic responsibilities. Review the Job Posting carefully and discuss the exact duties and responsibilities with the AD. The positions of artistic associate and resident director are often less formal, but provide a home base for a few months each season, opportunities to direct, and perhaps to head a project or festival, along with fewer producing or management responsibilities. Again, ask for clarity about the theatre's commitment to you and their expectations regarding your residency to them.

Some professional theatre directors will pursue producing or directing in related media and entertainment fields, such as television and cable, online series, films, and commercials. Working in these fields often requires additional training or an apprenticeship, because these industries are highly specialized and intensely competitive. Other directors might pursue coaching or conservatory and faculty appointments, especially when they have a passion for training and nurturing the next generation of theatre artists. Many of today's universities and conservatories expect their teachers who are professional artists to continue to work in their field, recognizing the value of such work to students, graduates, and the school's reputation. Most schools now treat your professional work as the equivalent of academic research or publishing. These organizations will work to accommodate professional schedules and pursuits. When you interview or apply for these positions, verify the individual program's practice towards professional work. Not only do these teaching positions come with a salary, but they can also provide healthcare and retirement benefits far better than those in the professional theatre field.

There are also many positions outside the field that need and would welcome your directing talents, experience, and skills, including your ability to lead collaborative teams, find innovative solutions, and achieve "on time delivery." Such jobs include producing or directing trade shows, client events, training sessions, conferences, and all-company meetings for corporations or fundraising galas and events for many charitable organizations. Directors have also set up small companies to provide the "entertainment" at these events. If you are a strong writer or editor, you may find lucrative work in writing grant applications, business plans, correspondence, press releases, etc. Some directors coach executives and attorneys in effective presentation skills; find work as personal assistant to a prominent artist, entertainer, or director; manage a restaurant or entertainment venue; stage rock-n-roll concerts, etc. My early directing career was subsidized by writing business materials, specifically for high-level executives in multi-national corporations. I spent the first five years of my freelance directing career across North America directing each day, but then writing speeches, memos, letters, and reports for a couple of CEOs at night.

There are many other activities that you can pursue to extend your contacts and spread your reputation in the field, such as becoming active in the directing unions or foundations, working for theatrical or performing arts causes that are important to you, or reading new plays for a theatre or a playwright's organization. Many theatres and other not-for-profits now hire "teaching artists" to develop community-created work, bring theatre to schools, or use drama to teach many subjects, from anatomy to algebra. Directors often manage or lead these efforts.

Directing in London and New York

The advantages of directing in New York or London (or any major urban center with dozens of theatres such as Chicago) are obvious: each is an undisputed center of professional theatre, with many remarkable (and available) artists and a heightened exposure for your work. Many more theatre professionals can see your work than they can in subsidized theatres in regional cities, and your productions may attract national media and press. The professional opportunities are remarkable, but the expenses of living in these cities are steep and the quality of life may be lower.

If you are lucky enough to be invited to direct at a "high-profile" theatre (e.g., Alameida, Royal Court, Young Vic, Signature Theatre, Public Theatre, Second Stage, etc.) you should understand the specific pressures on these organizations in an intensely competitive market. During my first directing job at an esteemed Off-Broadway theatre, the entire cast and staff of the theatre seemed to become agitated and anxious the day we moved into the theatre. After thinking I had done something wrong, I realized the problem was rooted in the acting company. As we moved towards performances, the stakes increased enormously. I believe, consciously or not, the actors were thinking, "This show needs to be the next big step in my career." Given the prominence of the theatre, the advance press interest in the show, and the unpredictability of the acting profession, this reaction was understandable. After a couple of previews, the anxiety level dropped as they re-discovered the power of the script and their performances.

Stranger still was the reaction of a few staff members. As is typical Off-Broadway, we had 4 weeks in rehearsal, tech and dress, 5 weeks in previews, and 4 weeks after the official opening. The artistic director seemed pleased with the show, but in the last ten days of previews, I received multiple calls from a handful of staff members, letting me know when the critic from *The New York Times* was attending and where he would be sitting. I was baffled, because we had finished rehearsing the production (with the blessing of the artistic director). Nevertheless, I watched the show the night before, met with the actors, and gave a handful of notes. A fellow director told me that the staff's behavior was an extreme example of the stress put on a not-for-profit theatre. The *New York Times* critic strongly affects ticket sales in a city with so much theatrical competition. A bad review can damage a show's future. Much to my dismay, I discovered a few years later that some of my fellow artistic directors would commit to producing a new play after its New York premiere, but then read negative or mixed reviews of the production and withdraw their interest.

The next time I directed in New York, I was prepared. Before we moved to the theatre, I reviewed our artistic vision and the remarkable work that we had accomplished in the studio. When the expected anxiety appeared during tech, I followed the advice of my colleague Sam Buntrock (best known for directing the

Menier Chocolate Factory revival of *Sunday in the Park with George*, which transferred to the West End and Broadway) who advised adopting a calm but confident demeanor and waiting for the storm to pass. Eventually, the anxiety ran its course, and everyone turned back to the director for help.

Life on the road

Many of us will grow weary of living out of a suitcase. And all of us will find ourselves out-of-work at times. At these times it is useful to review your personal and professional priorities and goals. This practice requires reflection and help from colleagues and close friends. Two fundamental questions are both simple and difficult to answer.

1 How well is your directing career (not this one rough patch) feeding you artistically and financially?
2 Are you thriving as a human being and as an artist?

Many of us delay having a home, committing to a serious relationship, or having a family in pursuit of artistic achievement and/or career success. Some of us achieve notable success, but the energy and sacrifice it takes may not be sustainable. However, avoid the most dangerous temptation of all—comparing your career success to that of your friends, colleagues, or classmates. This can lead to envy and a unwarranted sense of injustice that isolates you, and results in dwelling on the negative which often leads to bitterness. Condescension and chronic complaining will sour any rehearsal room. Remember that the theatre and the entertainment industries are notoriously fickle. Instead, reflect on the joy, wonder, and fulfillment you have found in the theatre. Recall the artists and audiences that you have affected through your directing career. Recognize the value of, and the need for, theatre in today's world.

If you can no longer withstand the uncertainty of the field, look for another opportunity in theatre, the arts, or out in the world for a period of time. As a wise writer once told me, "Life and art are journeys into the unknown—that's their wonder and their agony." As humans, we like to believe we can control our futures. We can't. That's especially difficult for directors, because we control so much in the rehearsal room.

Have patience and be kind to yourself.

9

Directing New Plays and Musicals

New plays and new musicals create the future of the theatre. If classics remind us of humankind's enduring tragedies and follies, then new works are snapshots of "now" and illuminate today's follies and tragedies. At best, these plays reveal the world around us in startling and compelling ways. In addition, they renew the art form. Directing world premieres of musicals and plays has brought me many thrilling personal and professional high points in my career. If you're especially lucky, you may direct a new play that becomes a classic of tomorrow. Of course, most new plays don't succeed, some have moderate success, and a few have widespread success. Leading the development of a new play is thrilling, invigorating, terrifying, and gratifying. For a director, new works require you to adjust your process to fulfill the writer's vision, but your role often expands to include collaborating on the evolution of the script as well as guiding the premiere production.

Understanding the rights of playwrights

To avoid confusion, it's important for every director to know the rights of a writer. By contract and common practice, the playwright owns and controls her work. She retains the copyright for her script, which is very different from the video industries, where writers assign their copyrights to a studio or production company. In the theatre, the playwright also retains considerable rights during development, including:

- **Script Approval**. No one can make changes of any sort to the script, including the title, lines, lyrics or words, or cuts, without the playwright's prior consent.
- **Artistic Approval**. The playwright has the right to approve the cast, the director, and the designers. In the case of a musical, add the choreographer, the music director, the orchestrator, and the arranger.
- **Right to Attend**. The playwright has the right to attend all casting sessions, rehearsals, previews, and performances.
- **Ownership of Incidental Contributions**. The playwright owns all approved revisions, suggestions, and contributions to the script made by others (i.e., director, actors, designers, dramaturg, etc.).
- **Royalties and Options**. The playwright will receive royalties on ticket sales, owns the subsidiary rights (i.e., film, TV, or other media) and has approval of any future options (i.e., Broadway, West End, Las Vegas, etc.). Sometimes the playwright agrees to pay a percentage of future royalties to the theatre premiering her work for a certain length of time (such as 5 percent of her royalties for 3–5 years).

After the premiere and first few professional productions of a new play, a writer may or may not continue to exert tight control over her script, but she retains the authority to do so. The unions representing playwrights are the Writers' Guild of Great Britain (WGGB) and the Dramatists Guild of America (DG) in the US.

Typical cycle of development

Obviously, the first step is the playwright writing the play. If she's fortunate, it's a commission from a theatre or producer. Commission agreements stipulate terms and obligations for both the writer and the theatre. These can include fees, proposed draft deadlines, possible workshops and public readings, royalties, and the theatre's First Right of Refusal—to produce the world premiere or release the rights after a specified date. Once the playwright submits the first draft to the theatre, its artistic/literary staff will read it, ask questions, and make suggestions. The writer decides which notes are useful and often writes another draft. The next step is hearing the play read aloud in some way—from a very informal reading to a workshopped public reading as part of a new play festival or program. However, multiple readings can lead to a play being "workshopped to death"—that is, endlessly revised and read aloud without receiving a full production. This is especially hard on writers, because certain theatres will workshop and read many new plays, but produce only a few. These plays are selected and optioned for production. After premiering, some will have additional productions, and a few will be produced in New York or London, which may lead to multiple regional performances in rep theatres across the country. A precious few will prove the very best new theatre of our time, becoming extraordinary works of art that change our field and/or affect the world.

The director's role

What is the director's role in [the] process of development? "To help the writer create the truest version of their vision of the play. The best way to do that is to ask really good questions."

Robert Schenkkan[1]

As the above quote indicates, directing new works requires you to develop and nurture a collaborative, trusting relationship with the playwright or composer and librettist. Your first task is to read the play and study it the way you would any other script, but you must also look for the playwright's inspiration, intentions, and vision for the play. Your job is not to tell the playwright how you want her to change the script; nor is it to rewrite the ending or anything else; it is to help and guide her in finding the most creative and powerful version of her script. No matter what level of the development process you are directing (e.g., cold reading, workshop and public reading, or premiere production), your North Star is the playwright's vision. Bear in mind that her vision may change frequently, as the play evolves in rehearsal and you experiment with interpretations or staging. And your process must adjust to the needs of the new work—essentially a work in continuous change—all the way up to opening night. If you prefer a deliberative and carefully controlled approach to rehearsal, such as one that ensures consistency in performances, don't direct new works! They demand very specific skill sets—the director must be deft, flexible, inventive, and decisive.

Working on new plays also requires a willingness to change, revise, try new ideas, and "play" from the actors and stage manager. If you direct the world premiere, the same applies to your designers, production staff, and crews. Therefore, cast the show with actors who enjoy adapting and changing their performance at any time, and create a rehearsal process in which everyone expects and welcomes new ideas and approaches. The playwright and you will be introducing a series of changes throughout the process, including new scenes, deletion of sections, new lines, changes in the order of scenes, and even the addition or deletion of characters. You may be restaging various scenes in the play many times to find the best solution. At the same time, a director must establish and maintain a safe, creative space for the playwright, by managing the constant flow of suggestions, notes, or requests for changes from the actors, the staff, the artistic director or producer, and even the playwright's agent. You should never keep these comments from the playwright, but you may need to translate the useful insights into staging ideas or possible solutions. If this sounds like a thankless task, think again. It's part high-wire act, part improvization and part discovery, but it also means that you are one of the principal artistic "parents" of a new theatrical experience.

In truth, very few playwrights try to control the rehearsal process. They tend to encourage collaboration, and welcome ideas for improving the script and the show. They rely upon your skill as a director to envision a production and value your talent and insight in bringing their creation to life. The rehearsal process often resembles a trek into the unknown— as the playwright, you, and the company work to discover the play's heart and soul.

> I love directors who make space for others and who nurture the unique qualities of a performer. Theater is so idiosyncratic and specific; I love being able to celebrate the fact that we are in this particular space at this particular time with these particular actors. Also, I love directors who are specific in their notes and aren't afraid to toss out ideas. Some writers may find this too proscriptive, but I like being able to at least have an opinion to agree or disagree with. Hearing their opinion helps me to better shape what I think.
>
> Lauren Yee[2]

There are many other tasks for the director on a new play. These include discovering the structure of the play, interviewing the playwright about her specific intentions, and the hoped-for effect of each scene, character, or moment in the play. In production, the director and designers must invent staging and design solutions to realize the written ideas, and the director must find a revelatory style of theatrical storytelling that best fits the script. Although the playwright is the foundational artist, it is the director who must turn her unknown and untested script into a performance. A director must advocate for, challenge, support, and nurture this script, while engaging authentically with its creator.

Directing new plays or musicals brings many directors their first professional jobs. To make that happen, you must have nurtured several positive relationships with playwrights or musical teams (composer, lyricist, and book writer). If you don't have any such relationships, find the writers and composers whose work most interests you. In the early part of your career, focus on young or emerging playwrights and musical teams. Research their existing and upcoming projects. Attend workshops, readings, or premieres of their new work, and stay for any talkbacks or receptions to meet the creators and hopefully begin a conversation. Also, attend showcases, festivals, or conferences where multiple new musicals and plays are being read/sung or performed. Check the calendars of organizations solely devoted to supporting playwrights or musical teams in development. Don't forget to include your classmates and fellow graduates of your university or conservatory program who create musicals or plays. You will be learning the wide array of new writing in today's theatre and extending your network of playwrights, dramaturgs, artistic directors, and theatres.

Working with the playwright

If you have a relationship with a writer, you may receive a draft of a new play directly from the playwright for your comment and interest. Or a theatre may send you a script for consideration. If you haven't worked with the playwright previously, the theatre will set up a meeting or conversation with the playwright, in hopes of getting her approval for you to direct a reading or production. Read the draft as you would any play, as described in Chapter 2. Jot down your first impressions. What do you love or admire in the script? What excites or fascinates you about the play? What works and doesn't work for you? Read the script again, and note the most important moments, scenes, and events. Make a list of questions and comments for the playwright. When you meet, tell her how excited you are about her script—communicate your genuine passion and interest in the work. Find out her reasons for creating the piece and try to understand the play from her point-of-view. Ask questions about anything you didn't understand in the script. Tell her any areas you think could use work or revisions. Ask lots of questions. Ask the playwright what she wants to focus on during the workshop/reading or production. If she is still searching for an opportunity to workshop/read the play, discuss contacts you both have that might show interest. According to *American Theatre* magazine, not counting *A Christmas Carol* or the plays of Shakespeare, the most produced playwright in the US in 2017–18 season was Lauren Gunderson (*Book of Will, The Revolutionists, I and You, Miss Bennet, Silent Sky*, among others.). She advises any director of a new play to always "ask where the climax of the play is. It sounds so basic and elemental that you might risk exposing yourself, but what you are really doing is aligning your vision with your playwright's. I think having a frank conversation about this with a playwright is critical to ensuring that you are on the same page from the start. If you think the climax is one moment and your playwright wrote it to be another, how can you build a play with a journey that culminates meaningfully? So. What is a climax? The deciding moment of the play's end that reveals the point of the whole journey. The critical decision, the critical revelation, the exposure of the character's true self … have this conversation early and perhaps often (plays change in rehearsal!). Ask 'what is the peak of this play's action?' 'What exact moment are we leading to?' 'Where is this play leading?' 'What moment exposes our character's true self and true journey?'"

Directing workshops and readings

Readings and workshops take many forms, including:

- A "cold reading" is what its name implies—actors read a script without rehearsal. A "table reading" also has limited time—playwright, director, dramaturg, actors, and staff sit around a table and read the latest script aloud, usually for the staff and a few invited guests.
- A "workshop reading" has a prescribed amount for rehearsal and reading(s). This can range from a couple of rehearsals to a week or two. The actors use music stands and read the script, and an additional actor reads the stage directions. For any reading, decide in advance what stage directions will be read—as few as possible! Eliminate

internal directives from the playwright that are intended for the actors, such as "sarcastic" or "sobbing." Keep the vital stage directions, such as "A gunshot" or "He destroys the furniture in his rage" that are necessary for the audience to understand the ongoing action. If you have time, listen to one reading of the script, correct mistakes or misread lines, clarify anything not understood, give direction only if any actor is interpreting the character or story incorrectly, and incorporate notes and revisions from the playwright.

If there are several rehearsals, encourage the playwright to talk about her inspiration, intentions, and vision in writing the play and answer specific questions about the script or a character's journey. Work with the actors to figure out the best overall approach to their characters, as well as paying attention to their most important events and moments in the play. While reviewing important scenes, keep an eye on the telling of the story—making sure the audience can understand what is happening. If you have time to help the actors sketch in their characters, find the moments for them to connect with their fellow performers— when they should turn and face each other, but also note times when they should face out so that the audience can hear a key point and see the actors' reactions. Keep the pace and flow of the scenes moving. Generally, don't ask the actors to memorize their lines, but do ask them to review important moments or sections to increase familiarity. Don't use props unless absolutely necessary—an actor's pencil can become a cigarette, a sword, or whatever you need. Resist design elements such as sound/music and lighting unless the theatre can provide them quickly and seamlessly and they significantly enhance the reading. The beauty of a public reading is that audiences invariably use their own imaginations to build the world of the play (adding their own visuals, sets, costumes, effects, sounds, and music) while they focus on the story. Fundamentally, you are mounting a quick sketch of the script, so that the playwright, the theatre or producer, the dramaturg (and you), can glimpse what the play might be in performance. As you rehearse for the reading, set up regular times with your playwright and the stage management or literary staff for revisions to be printed for the cast and yourself. In rehearsals, review the changes aloud with the actors and the playwright. Blocking should be minimal and usually only consists of navigating the music stands and figuring out where to place the scripts.

- A "staged reading" is a partially or fully staged version of the work. If you're lucky enough to have a "staged reading" or a "workshop production" for a musical, work with the entire creative team to schedule time to learn the music and stage whatever scenes you (or the choreographer) are going to use as a demonstration of singing, dancing, acting, storytelling, and audience impact the piece will have in a fully realized production. Musicals and commercial productions often hold a series of public or invited readings—often referred to as "backer's auditions," in hopes of attracting the additional investors or producing partners needed to mount a full production.

Casting for workshops and readings is often a very quick process. Frequently the theatre, the playwright, and you will agree on actors to hire without auditions. You and the playwright should decide which roles are most important to the reading—in acting ability, type, age, ethnicity, special skill, etc. Focus on those roles in casting. For the others, work with the theatre to cast good performers who can pull off the acting, even though they may not be exactly right for the part. As mentioned before, try your best to cast actors who are daring, flexible, lively, quick to take notes, and excited to work on a new play. You are asking them to pull a performance out of their hats and deal with the constant script changes and rewrites, which can keep coming until minutes before the reading. Casting an actor whose process is slow or studied or who is anxious or frustrated with changes will hamper the process and prevent the reading from achieving its full potential.

After each rehearsal, spend time with the playwright discussing the progress of the day, the actors' work, any comments, or questions that you, the dramaturg, or the playwright may have. Express your opinions, make suggestions or ask for revisions, and listen carefully to the playwright. Always verify that you are both "on the same page." Use your skills and expertise to direct the reading, but resist the temptation to "prove your directing talent" to the playwright, the theatre, or the producer. Inevitably, seeking to impress leads a director to push the actors towards results, which deprives the reading of their insights and spontaneity. It also reduces the time they have left to integrate the revisions and create a character.

After any public reading, congratulate the playwright and thank the actors. Take time to review the reading, the audience reactions, the acting, and the discoveries made with the playwright, dramaturg, literary manager, and artistic director. Ask the playwright what she wants to work on next with the script. If you are excited about the piece and/or working with the writer, and see further potential and promise in the script, you will want to direct future readings and the world premiere. Tell the playwright first, then the artistic director, producer, and staff. If you are no longer excited about the script, or the path it's taking, be respectful but straightforward with the playwright (and theatre) in withdrawing.

If you are a young or emerging director, the theatre or producer may not hire you to direct the premiere, even if your work was excellent on the reading. There are many reasons for this, such as the playwright works frequently with another director, the playwright or her agent wants a more prominent director, the theatre works with a regular group of experienced directors, or the artistic director wants to direct the show himself. You will probably never know, but try not to take it personally. Keep in touch with the playwright and the theatre, and attend a performance when the show premieres. Keep in mind that as your reputation grows as a strong developer/director of new work, the time will come when you will be the first choice.

Directing the world premiere

You are asked to direct the world premiere. Congratulations! You will follow the same preparation and planning that you would for any production, however, every step will always involve the playwright. Continue or begin (if you didn't direct the workshop) conversations with the playwright and the theatre. Keep the communication open with the playwright concerning her ongoing script development. Will she be making revisions before the rehearsals begin? Ask the artistic director, literary head, and dramaturg for their thoughts and hopes for the script and the production. Include the playwright in every step of your pre-production process, from developing your concept, to selection of designers, to the director/design conference, and to the casting of actors. For instance, playwrights must be invited to all auditions and callbacks and approve every offer. For a musical, the audition room can become very crowded, with the presence of the composer, lyricist, book writer, producer, director, choreographer, music director, accompanist, and reader, among others. However, in casting, pursue the best actor for each part; assemble the actors who will best fill the playwright's vision. Many creators will rely upon your judgment as the director to handle many of these tasks—from design development to casting, but they must be informed and approve choices before decisions are made.

Unless you have significant prior work experience with the playwright, decide in advance who gives which notes to the company before rehearsals begin. Ask and expect the playwright to provide the invaluable information in rehearsal on the source of the play, the characters, their backgrounds and intentions, as well as to elucidate the function of each scene in the overall play. However, she should give all acting and production notes to you, which you will communicate to the cast and creative team. She should not be directing in rehearsals. At the same time, you should set up and manage a process that works for the playwright regarding notes, suggestions, ideas, and requests for lines revisions or cuts from the actors. The playwright may or may not want direct feedback from the actors. Engage the dramaturg or literary staff (and if needed, the artistic director) of the theatre in this process of revision and comments. It's not that you control the revision and improvement of the script; rather, you provide a more structured process for discovery, revision, and improvement—one that helps the playwright and her script. When the playwright is not present, make very clear your process for questions or suggestions for changes. All such questions and suggestions should go through you and the dramaturg, and then be passed along to the playwright. A good rule of thumb in the rehearsal room is stating your expectation, such as "Make what's written now work better and better. You don't get to rewrite the play. Figure it out."

Meet with the dramaturg or literary staff regularly, so that you are in agreement regarding the script, the moments that are not landing or working, and any suggestions for revisions. Although I establish an open and collaborative rehearsal room, new plays and musicals often require more structure. If everyone is asking for changes or giving suggestions about the script, the playwright may become overwhelmed and defensive. You will also notice during workshops and readings each playwright's process of rewrites and changes. Some are quick and deft, turning out revisions or new scenes with speed; others need more time; others rewrite and listen to several versions of a scene before they find the best one. Whenever possible, adapt the rehearsals to the writer's process.

Rarely does a playwright have the time to be present throughout the entire rehearsal period; she is likely working on other scripts, premier productions, or projects. That said, it's often healthier for everyone if she attends at several key times during the process and stays away at others. In advance, discuss with the playwright and the theatre the plans for her to be present in rehearsals. Ideally, the playwright will be present at the first read-through and table work to talk about her ideas, answer questions, provide character or story background, listen to the play aloud, and revise as necessary. Once you begin blocking and scene work, it's useful to have time in rehearsal without the constant presence of the playwright. Once you reach the stage of run-throughs, it's very important to have the playwright present. As the performances start to take shape and the storytelling improves, the playwright can see her script anew and often make important revisions. After that, the playwright returns at some point in tech and stays until opening.

Also, as the pace of rehearsals picks up, your job is to make the rewrites work. If you don't agree with the playwright's notes or revisions or cuts—if they seem to undercut what she had said she's working towards—talk with her and mention your thoughts to the dramaturg and artistic director. Ask lots of questions, but focus them—dig for the playwright's intention and vision of particular moments, lines, or scenes. Try to steer her towards more productive rewrites, while supporting her vision.

Occasionally playwrights will want the script acted and staged **exactly** as written and resist revisions or suggestions. Whatever the reason, they become inflexible or stubborn about any changes. This can happen when a playwright is inexperienced or insecure, or has spent far too much time having her plays workshopped to death, trying to incorporate each theatre's notes but never landing a production. Of course, they are not legally required to make any changes. If you meet with resistance, your best tactic is to ask lots of questions, try different approaches to problematic lines or scenes, state your opinion to the playwright but keep the conversation going. Enlist the dramaturg—and even the artistic director—if you're in agreement about what needs to be done. Manage the number of people making comments in the room. Of course, the other extreme can happen, too. If a playwright becomes overly collaborative regarding the script—asking for comments, suggestions, and ideas from everyone in the company—she may write for the actors and not her play. In such cases, speak to the playwright and encourage her to defer a decision to make a change until you, the dramaturg, and she can review them.

Playwrights want to see the production appear not simply as they envisioned it, but better. If the level of talent in the room is high, playwrights jump at making the play better, based upon the creative work of so many artists. They value your artistry, leadership, and knowledge in bringing the play to life. Your job is to keep trying to discover a better and more authentic (truer) version of her vision of the play.

In my experience, a new play can **always** use more rehearsal time and additional previews to find its best performance. More time allows you to try different versions or scenes, lines, and directorial approaches both in rehearsal and in front of live audiences. Previews are especially useful in clarifying the strengths and weaknesses of the play script and observing its effect on audiences. Keep talking and suggesting changes, but constantly question yourself. When a moment or scene doesn't work, is it the acting, the directing, the concept, or the writing? Notice that I put "the writing" last, to remind you not to jump to the conclusion that it's the writing. Discuss with the playwright in advance how you and she think the rehearsals for previews should best be used. For musicals of epic scale and size or high complexity, you may need to keep making revisions until the last minute of rehearsal on opening day. This requires deft, brave writing by the creative team and very persuasive, quick, and decisive direction on your part as the time is short and the pressures are high. Union agreements require changes and revisions to stop after opening night. However, for commercial productions travelling to various cities before the West End or Broadway, the contract may be set up for constant revisions on the road until opening night on Broadway.

Devotion to new work

I have been able to work with a battery of incredible directors. These wonderful experiences have left me in awe of the job a good director does in bringing a play to life. In my opinion, there is NO decision a playwright makes regarding their work that is more important than the choice of who directs it ... My one cardinal rule is that [the director has] to genuinely love my play. That sounds like a minor request, but I don't believe it is. Work is work, and directors must line up a lot of it to make ends meet ... I try my best to only align myself with directors who have come to my work due to a real connection. The only way I can have the necessary amount of trust to step away and leave my play in their hands is by believing that the work means almost as much to them as it does to me. That way, they'll fight (when needed) to prevent compromises that would damage the play's execution. In addition to being the "air-traffic controller" between all of the disparate theatre elements (actors, stage design, lighting, sound), the director is also a much-needed second set of dramaturgical eyes as my play gets up and on its feet.

Kemp Powers[3]

Developing and producing new work requires a considerable amount of effort, time and expense, and it's demanding for all involved. For the theatre, a new play may require multiple workshops or readings prior to being produced. In production, additional artistic staffing and support may be needed to deal with the changes, but also to cover extra needs for design, specialized elements, casting, musical arrangements, copying, orchestrations, etc. A theatre's dedication to (or obsession with) world premieres carries its own risks, because many new plays only find their true voice and artistic potential after additional productions. For example, the remarkable plays of August Wilson enjoyed great benefits from an extended series of co-productions at half a dozen regional theatres around the US, before heading to Broadway. For the director, the workshop and development process can take months, with modest compensation. However, the playwright or composer, lyricist, and librettist have the biggest challenges—finding the time and resources to create a new piece of theatre from scratch.

Most of all, directing new plays requires a love of playwrights and new theatre. It takes a passionate devotion to the promise of a new theatrical story. Working on a new play or musical is both invigorating and terrifying, but I count these experiences as blessings, because they demand so much collaboration, invention, courage, and artistry from everyone—especially the playwright and the director. I hope your career will bring you many opportunities to direct new musicals or plays.

10

Nurturing Your Art and Yourself

For directors, it's easy to become consumed in the constant race to find work, promoting ourselves, and feverishly trying to stay in contact with dozens of people who may hire or help us. By personality, directors are typically goal-oriented and obsessively focused on projects, which works well in mounting a show, but not so well in our personal lives. We often overlook the need to nurture our artistry and to take care of ourselves. All of us must find our own ways of inspiring the artist within and sustaining ourselves as human beings. These efforts prove invaluable during the fallow times that every director faces during a career. In my experience, building a successful career and becoming a master director can only happen when we also nurture our artistry and our personal life. Ironically, the best times to do so are often when we are unemployed or working outside the theatre. Therefore, we must learn to view fallow periods as opportunities not as punishments or rebukes. There are several useful ways to cultivate your artistry and improve your personal life, including:

- **Close friends and trusted colleagues**. Push aside your detailed "communications, networking, and contacts plan" and take time to nurture close friendships inside and outside the theatre. People who work in other professions often offer new perspectives on our jobs. They admire us for "doing what we love," but also view directing as simply a job. Close friends provide a caring, grounding force in our lives. As you work with favored colleagues, build closer relationships with those you trust. Avoid colleagues who are especially negative or competitive. Meet and connect with your close friends and trusted colleagues regularly.
- **Don't hide when you don't have work!** This will isolate you and you can easily lose perspective on your talent, contributions, and the

achievements in your career. Of course, you will be asked awkward questions: "What are you directing?" "What's next?" Don't give in to embarrassment or self-criticism. Every freelance theatre artist is regularly unemployed. Give a short reply, but then talk about what you're doing that excites you. Or what you've seen or experienced that's fascinating (and not only in the theatre). Keep attending the shows of your mentors, advocates, and colleagues.

- **Stay active in your union.** Volunteer for committees, projects, and causes important at Equity or SDC. Look for panels, speakers, seminars, and programs for members. Attend events, annual meetings, speakers' series, and regional gatherings, including at any of the advocacy or service organizations, such as Stage Directors UK or TCG.

- **Adjust the results you are aiming for.** When we begin directing, we're focused on getting a gig—any gig. As we mature, we can become fixated on what we want to direct and at what theatre and at what level of the industry. This is a short step away from believing we have failed if we don't achieve all three. Change it up. Widen the scope of what you aspire to direct and focus less on a specific theatre or the "level" of theatre you think should be hiring you.

- **Explore other genres and types of theatre.** For instance, playwriting for children and young people has become very sophisticated, complex, and progressive in many countries, including in the US and the UK. Check out the professional children's companies. And look at the website for ASSITEJ, the International Organization for Youth Theatre. Attend and research "documentary" theatre, created by artists or companies that create a play from interviews, written testimonies, and writings of the people involved in crises or conflicts in their communities. Look for the theatre works you don't know well but which appear interesting.

- **Explore the uses of theatre arts beyond the four walls of a theatre.** Many "teaching" or "citizen artists," collectives, and companies use the techniques of the theatre to reach at-risk, underserved, disenfranchised, or forgotten communities. For example, they use play or musical creation to give voice to veterans suffering from PTSD, to pensioners and retirees cut off from the outside world, to undocumented immigrants and deportees, to prisoners, differently abled, or to stroke or trauma victims. Theatrical storytelling is a remarkable way for people to share their stories, find creative expression, and uncover deep wounds. The act of expressing one's story through theatre is often therapeutic and sometimes life-changing.

- **Try something new in theatre**. Write a play. Act in a reading or a production. Shadow a scenic designer. Interview artists for your own blog.
- Figure out what specifically restores your energy and vitality. Is it extra sleep or extra physical activity? Rock climbing or working out? Dinner with your partner or children, watching documentaries, or social media? Meeting up with friends or colleagues? Make it a practice to choose activities to stay vital.
- **Find things that are absorbing and fascinating which have nothing to do with the theatre**. Explore activities, hobbies, and endeavors that fascinate you. For me, it's designing and making clock faces, hands, and cases as well as sports photography. The best practice is to choose an activity or interest that is so compelling that you lose track of time.
- **Structure your days when you're not working**. Set a finite amount of time you spend chasing work, promoting yourself, or networking. Make a calendar of regular meals, physical exercise, chores, and annual check-ups with doctors, dentists, etc. Write to the friend or relative you've been meaning to, or call your parents. Make your social interactions a priority. As you create the working environment for the rehearsal room, create one for yourself in your home or office.
- As your directing career ebbs and flows, jot down personal lists. What do you want to do when you have free time? What would you find inspiring or fascinating? Is it watching the entire filmography of a cinema director? Is it going to a baseball game or a football (US or UK) match, a spoken-word poetry festival, a political rally or protest, or attending a late-night event at the Tate Gallery? A rock concert or a music festival? Do you want to visit the "manuscript" collections of museums, such as the Karpeles Manuscript Library Museum (11 locations in the US), the British Library's Collection of George III at the King's Library in its new St. Pancras building, or the Smithsonian Museum in Washington, DC?
- **Read voraciously**. Anything—fiction or non-fiction. Feed your curiosity. If you want to read plays, read what's fascinating and inspiring to you. Read all the plays written by Caryl Churchill, Tony Kushner, Harold Pinter, or Sarah Ruhl. Over time, do you want to see the entire *American Century Cycle* of August Wilson? Or read his poetry (it was

his first writing discipline before he took up drama). As a Shakespeare director (and stage combat choreographer), I took an afternoon on a day off to visit The Wallace Collection in London, because it houses an extraordinary collection of European and Oriental Arms and Armory.

- **Observe the world**. Travel as much as you can afford. If you can't afford to travel, visit public spaces in your own city. Not the tourist sites, but the neighborhoods, bars, sports events, political rallies, street fairs, community centers, places of worship, and markets in communities that you don't know. Watch people. Talk with people. Find out what makes them tick. One of my favorite quotes on directing and on inspiration comes from Jim Jarmusch (the acclaimed independent film director of *Permanent Vacation*, *Stranger than Paradise*, and *Broken Flowers*, among others):

> Nothing is original. Steal from anywhere that resonates with inspiration or fuels your imagination. Devour old films, new films, music, books, paintings, photographs, poems, dreams, random conversations, architecture, bridges, street signs, trees, clouds, bodies of water, light and shadows. Select only things to steal from that speak directly to your soul. If you do this, your work (and theft) will be authentic. Authenticity is invaluable; originality is non-existent. And don't bother concealing your thievery—celebrate it if you feel like it. In any case, always remember what Jean-Luc Godard said: "It's not where you take things from—it's where you take them to."[1]

Throughout it all, keep in mind the "Artist's Journey." The evolution and progression of an artist to mastery can take years. It's often a winding, arduous and wonderful path. A colleague, Bill Partlan (an accomplished director, especially of new plays and musicals, an artistic director of regional theatres, and now Associate Professor/Head of Directing at Arizona State University), describes the journey of a director and artist:

> The greatest challenge is having enough life experience, and experience working with actors and designers to feel truly embedded in the process. To be confident that even if you don't have answers, you can find them along the way. It takes years of experience to get to a place where you can tackle almost every piece and do it justice.

Partlan goes on to suggest that these experiences bring an ability to take the show beyond just the script and the staging.

> Most directors start out by very carefully figuring out where and when everyone moves, (like) an entire traffic pattern. For early directors, that's their

safety net . . . It's when you get to that place where you've maybe done that, but you can put it aside and trust your instincts to see where it goes, that's the big step . . . That's when things get very interesting, and usually where the best work is done. Theater is a sum of its parts that's greater than any of those parts.[2]

Part IV

Becoming an Artistic Director

11

Leading a Theatre . . . or Not

Many directors aspire to become artistic directors. Many do not. Early in your career, artistic direction can appear to be the definition of career success. We believe the job will give us the power, resources, and opportunity to create extraordinary art, advance the entire theatre field, create a lasting and important legacy, and perhaps even change the world. After directing productions at several professional theatres, we learn that these jobs are absorbing, fulfilling, and rewarding, but also that they are more complicated and challenging than we previously thought. Certainly, these positions have prestige and power within the field. Without exception every director yearns to decide what show she directs. As artistic director, you will get to pick the shows and the directors!

Those who aspire to artistic direction have many powerful professional and personal motives. You may be passionate about developing and premiering new plays or musicals, or producing shows with social, political, and economic resonance. You may want to produce Western European or American classics; contemporary or modern works; cross-disciplinary performances; immersive/interactive experiences; or performances created by, in, and for specific communities. You may want to take action on issues of "Equity, Diversity and Inclusion." In the US, "EDI" is an industry-wide initiative that seeks to actively address and dismantle the systemic discrimination and historical imbalance in opportunity, equal pay, and access in the hiring of women, artists of color, LBGTQ artists, etc., at all levels of the professional theatre. If you're devoted to nurturing the next generation of professional artists, do you want to lead an organization that both produces professional theatre and trains artists, managers, and craftspeople for the field? Being an artistic director can give you the opportunity to realize such goals.

After many years on the road, freelance directors tire of the constant travel, of living out of a suitcase, of departing immediately after opening night and never watching the show grow (or not), and knowing little about the audiences' reactions over the course of the run. In addition, the freelance director's constant travel and work schedule can complicate or damage relationships and create a sense of dislocation or disconnection. As we mature, it becomes a priority to find steady jobs with reliable income and benefits, including healthcare (US) and retirement savings accounts or pensions. Personal relationships become more important, especially if you want to have, or do have, children. You may desire a home and a better quality of life that's not affordable in New York or London.

The job

The artistic director's job is exhilarating and demanding. It can be a deeply rewarding and fulfilling endeavor as you engage and inspire teams of artists, craftspeople, and managers to create theatre. You can also watch the impact of your work on the community in which you live, hold extended "conversations" with your artists and your audiences, and increase the theatre's impact locally, regionally, and nationally. Your efforts can lift a theatre to national prominence; you can create masterful new plays and musicals; and become a thoughtful leader in the field.

The role of an artistic director has changed considerably over the past 25 years. The "overhead" required today is substantial and significant and may demand too much sacrifice. "Overhead" refers to the increased institutional duties, responsibilities, and expectations that face today's artistic directors. These include managing staff and attending multiple meetings (e.g., Board committees, staff, marketing, development, etc.), creating short- and long-term strategic plans for programming and finances. In the first three to five years, the workload is enormous and all-consuming. An industry writer once asked me what was most surprising about the job that I had not anticipated. Without thinking, I said, "The wind never stops blowing." That is, the pace never diminishes. The 60–70-hour work week never stopped, though this was partly due to my artistic aspirations and ambitions for the theatre, including the creation of new initiatives and programs, but partly due to my responsibilities and duties beyond artistic direction. The managing director and I also faced the many large and small crises (e.g., meeting payroll, addressing unexpected repairs to the facility, losing rights to an upcoming play to a Broadway producer, or replacing artists). Solving these problems was often stimulating and gratifying, but also extremely time consuming and draining. On a cyclical basis, the budget required cuts that we tried to address with creative solutions. Although these cycles of challenges would be followed by thrilling cycles of growth and artistic achievement, the workload only increased with the addition of new programs and staff. And artistic directors always face overlapping cycles of producing and directing at the same time as planning for the next season which includes play selection, budgeting, scheduling, and hiring.

Let's take a moment to review the traditional definition of the job. In subsidized or not-for-profit theatres, an "artistic director" is the theatre company's leader who creates and articulates the artistic vision for the organization and then is responsible for achieving it. This includes the selection of programming, hiring (and firing) of all artists, heads of artistic and production staff, and often education. He produces and oversees all the artistic and production aspects of each show from title selection through closing night. The artistic director is responsible for establishing, maintaining, and advancing the standards of artistic achievement for all productions. To do so, he defines and demands whatever the level of "artistic quality" that he believes is most appropriate to each activity. In addition, the artistic director leads the theatre in the creation of new programming initiatives, community engagement projects, and innovative artistic events. He serves as the national (and sometimes international) representative and spokesperson for the company to the theatre field, including industry service organizations and the press and media. Typically, he will direct one or more productions for the theatre each season.

Over the past two decades, the duties and responsibilities of artistic directors in the US have increased exponentially, especially in fundraising. Today the artistic director is expected to personally take on significant fundraising "asks" of donors, nurture relationships with national foundations and government agencies; attend development and marketing events; develop personal relationships with trustees; and raise the national profile of the theatre. In addition, he is expected to possess the financial skills to prepare expense budgets for future seasons. Nevertheless, there's no creative job in theatre that I find more stimulating and rewarding.

Understanding mission and vision

If you want to become an artistic director, it's useful to know the ubiquitous language of strategic planning. In the past few decades, entire industries have been created to develop missions, visions, strategic plans, tactics, goals, and core values for corporate and not-for-profit organizations. Surprisingly, disagreement and confusion is widespread about the meaning of two key terms: mission and vision. In my view, a "mission" is an organization's *raison d'être*. It also describes what the institution does, whom it serves, and how it operates. In other words, a mission is an overview of the theatre's current state of operations and offerings. A "vision" is aspirational and forward-looking. It describes a visionary future for the theatre. In my experience, people (including donors) are far more eager to follow a vision than a mission. Many identify the vision as an organizational "North Star" for the staff, company, trustees, and the public. Jack Welch, the former CEO of General Electric, is widely quoted: "Good business leaders create a vision, articulate the vision, passionately own the vision, and relentlessly drive it to completion."[1] Today organizations often use mission and vision interchangeably, thereby diminishing the power of both. On the other hand, many theatres now create a mashup of both mission and vision to great effect—as a brief declaration of now and the future.

A "Strategic Plan" is a plan for achieving the artistic and institutional vision for an organization. It describes the changes, resources, and season-by-season goals over a defined period of time for the theatre's Board, staff, donors, and supporters. Many theatres also now adopt "Core Values" (also called beliefs, ethics, or principles) that support the mission, shape the internal culture and reflect what the company most values in the workplace.

As you develop interest in specific theatres, it's useful to explore these concepts on their websites. Evaluate the mission and vision for their clarity and uniqueness. Is the vision exciting, inspirational and bold? Is the mission consistent with the work of the theatre? Several not-for-profit regional theatres in the US use similar language, such as: "The mission of XYZ

Theatre is to provide artistically diverse theatrical experiences of the highest quality. XYZ Theatre also strives to serve, challenge, stimulate, and entertain while operating in a fiscally responsible manner." Added below is: "XYZ Theatre shares its resources with the community through education and outreach initiatives intended for a wide range of people with the goal of expanding and diversifying the audience while enriching the community." There is no accompanying "vision." Unfortunately, this mission statement is out-of-date, generic and vague. Every performing arts organization wants to produce work of the highest quality. What does "highest quality" mean? Who is creating the production, for what audience, and why? A vision statement can be more intentional or passionate but equally vague. For example, Theatre ABC seeks "to create empathy and understanding in our community" and address "the important issues facing our nation." How? Compare the examples above with the statements below. Note if these are missions or visions or a combination.

- "The Alliance Theatre will lead the national field by deeply engaging with its local community, modeling radical inclusion and catalytic experiences on our stages, in our classrooms, and throughout Atlanta."[2]
- "Inspired by Shakespeare's work and the cultural richness of the United States, we [Oregon Shakespeare Festival] reveal our collective humanity through illuminating interpretations of new and classic plays, deepened by the kaleidoscope of rotating repertory."[3]
- According to their website, "The Royal Court Theatre is the writers' theatre. It is the leading force in world theatre for energetically cultivating writers—undiscovered, emerging, and established. Through the writers, the Royal Court is at the forefront of creating restless, alert, provocative theatre about now. We open our doors to the unheard voices and free thinkers that, through their writing, change our way of seeing."[4]

For a theatre that interests you and is looking for new leadership, look up their mission, vision, and history and review them. How would you revise or reinvent the vision statement to make it more aspirational, dynamic, and relevant? Write down your ideas. Changing a mission statement of a theatre is a deliberative process, one that must include the Board, staff, and various stakeholders, but you will be expected to bring your **artistic vision** to any theatre interviewing you for artistic director.

Organizational structure

The most common industry practice in the subsidized/not-for-profit field is the model of "dual" leadership. In addition to an artistic director, the board of governors or trustees also interviews and hires a managing or executive director. The managing director hires his heads of staff (e.g., directors of development, marketing, etc.), and is responsible for all administrative/management functions, including negotiations and contracts, marketing and sales, communications, fundraising (also called development or advancement), maintenance and upkeep of facilities, IT, security, financial management and oversight, including budgeting, appropriate use of resources, and control of expenses and income. In practice, the managing director oversees day-to-day operations. In this dual leadership model, each leader reports directly and independently to the board of directors. However, the traditional understanding of the two roles is that the managing director's primary role is to support the vision of the artistic director.

This model of dual leadership works as both a division of labor and a system of checks and balances. The intention is to balance the artistic vision of the theatre with the financial and human resources of the institution. To achieve success, dual leadership requires an extraordinary partnership between the two leaders. Each is likely to have differing talents, working styles, ambitions, and personalities because the required training, expertise, and professional experience of each job is very different. This traditional model demands an authentic, committed, and respectful partnership. Each leader must earn and keep the trust of the other. The managing director must support and respect the artistic vision, and the artistic director must support and respect the managing director's efforts to grow resources, while protecting the health and viability of the entire organization. Such a vital, active, and significant relationship demands public solidarity, especially with trustees, but also with donors, the staff under each partner's supervision, and the theatre industry at large. An effective partnership of the two leaders resembles good parenting. Each must never allow anyone to divide and separate them, and each must always uphold the other's decisions in public. Michael Kaiser, the brilliant and enormously successful former Executive Director of The Kennedy Center, writes with humor and expertise about the challenges, tensions, and risks of failure in the model of the dual leadership on his blog.[5]

However, some boards of directors prefer a single leadership model for their theatre companies. The artistic single leader can be called Producing

Artistic Director, Executive Artistic Director, or The Director. A management single leader is often called Chief Executive Officer (CEO), President, or Executive Producer. This single leadership model reflects the Board's preference in running a theatre, and invariably alters the top priorities of the organization. In the extreme, one side is pursued at the expense of the other—business or art. A switch from dual to sole leadership can also happen in a crisis, such as the sudden death or firing of one leader, an unsustainable increase in accumulated debt, an economic downturn, or the discovery of malfeasance or misfeasance by staff. Change in leadership may also be initiated by a powerful chair, a significant donor, or a small group of trustees who want to push the theatre in a different direction because they disapprove of and doubt the current leader's vision.

At the Globe Theatre in London, Neil Constable serves as CEO, and the theatre's artistic director and general manager report directly to him. Following traditional corporate practice, Constable is also a full, voting member of the Board, but the two others are not. Rufus Norris is director of the Royal National Theatre (a term used historically at the organization) and its executive director reports directly to him, although neither serves as a full, voting member of the National's Board.

Learning from artistic directors

When you started directing in several theatres in different locations, you began to learn about differing artistic visions and the wide range of programming, resources, organizations, audiences, and community support at theatres across the country. As you move towards leading a theatre, you have a great source of information about artistic direction right in front of you—the artistic director. As you did with assistant directing, watch and learn the way he pursues his artistic vision, produces shows, and how he leads the organization. Take note of his strengths and weaknesses and his best and worst practices. Better yet, talk with him about the job, his experiences, approaches, and philosophies. What does he believe are the highest priorites of his job? What are the joys and hardships of the position? Depending on time available, most artistic directors are willing and happy to share their experiences, including the story of becoming an AD. Gaining an insider's view from several artistic directors is invaluable as you begin to form your own ideas for leading a theatre.

Explore and research

Following the industry websites, theatre publications and blogs, and social media sites is the best way to find out when an artistic directorship becomes vacant. Job posting sites (some require a fee) for theatres and the performing arts are also useful when looking for job announcements, but sometimes they don't list all of the significant positions that are open. You should check the websites of the individual theatres, the leading recruitment firms, industry media, and talk with your colleagues.

When you become interested in a specific theatre, attend a show there, if possible. Then begin some basic research into its operations, programming, leadership, artistic achievement, and budget:

- Review the bios of the current artistic and management directors.
- Check programs and press releases online to find out the names of the artists they hire.
- Check production photos to determine the level of production values.
- Explore the production and programming history of the theatre.
- Read the mission and vision statements. Evaluate and then compare them against the theatre's production history. Do they align with each other?
- Talk with friends or colleagues who have worked at the theatre.
- Review media stories and reviews. How much coverage do they receive from theatre media? How does the local and national theatre community view their work?

From freelance directing to artistic direction

Different artists have become artistic directors, including literary managers, playwrights, actors, designers, and producers, but the vast majority are professional directors. This makes sense, because the talents, experience, and expertise of a working director can easily transfer to the job of artistic director. There are several characteristics that can make you an appealing and competitive candidate, including:

- an established reputation for directing imaginative and exciting productions at other professional theatres of similar size and scale;

- prior directing success and positive internal reputation if you have worked for the theatre now looking;
- prior artistic, financial, and critical success in directing productions of similar type, style, or genre that the theatre produces (e.g., musicals, physically-based ensemble theatre, or new plays);
- a well-developed and robust network of theatre professionals, artists, and colleagues whom you could attract and hire to work at the theatre;
- experience as an associate artistic director, artistic producer, or resident director at a similar theatre;
- experience as an associate artistic director, artistic producer, or resident director at the theatre now recruiting. However, this is no guarantee of an interview. Trustees often do not seriously consider associate artistic directors or resident directors currently on the theatre's staff. Their decision can be based on several factors: the trustees want someone of higher stature and experience (e.g., someone with "West End" credits); they don't know what or how much you do within the organization; they don't want to hire anyone associated with the prior artistic director; or they don't know you personally. To help your chances of being interviewed and seriously considered, you should proactively nurture positive relationships with trustees, donors, and staff leaders across the organization from **the moment you are hired**;
- a very close match between your experiences, interests, and expertise and the Board's highest priorities for the new leader. However, examine carefully the premise that you are a close match to the required criteria. Have you worked at the theatre? Have you worked as a resident director or associate at a similar sized theatre? What experiences and skills make you an especially close match? Test your assumptions with a close colleague who you're confident will tell you the truth. If the theatre is seeking a new generation of leadership and artistic vision focused on new and contemporary plays, but your resumé is built on productions of American classics, there's a disconnect. If the theatre wants a new generation of leaders and a bold new direction, your reputation as a dynamic, engaging, and wildly innovative emerging director may attract high interest;
- sophisticated and mature interpersonal skills, especially in leadership, people skills, and communications. Boards are drawn to leaders with a strong capacity to inspire, excite, and engage many different groups of people, both inside and outside the theatre;

- knowledge of the theatre field and current trends in programming, funding, fieldwide initiatives, and commitments, such as the tremendous growth in foundation grants and individual contributions to support the commissioning, development, and production of new plays and musicals; the growth of immersive/experiential theatrical events; programming and marketing efforts to attract a new generation of audiences, such as millennials; the expansion of co-producing partnerships between groups of subsidized theatres; or the increasing practice of commercial producers financially "enhancing" productions at not-for-profit theatres as a try-out before a Broadway premier;
- good luck and good timing. No matter how talented or deserving you are, good luck and good timing can play a significant part. My first production at the Alabama Shakespeare Festival (ASF) was *On the Verge* by Eric Overmeyer (also a television writer and/or producer on *Homicide, Law & Order, The Wire, Boardwalk Empire, Treme, Bosch,* and *The Man in the High Castle*). Martin Platt, the Festival's Founder and Artistic Director hired me at the recommendation of David Crank, a colleague and friend who designed regularly at the theatre. Between the director/designer conference in December and the first rehearsal in February, Platt announced his resignation and the theatre began its national search. I was raised in the southern US, and knew the culture well. After three years of classical actor training in London, I had spent my early career leading a small, summer Shakespeare festival in Virginia. After moving to New York City, I had built my resumé and reputation by directing Shakespeare plays and other classics and developing new plays in workshops and directing premieres. My early directing was at small regional theatres, summer Shakespeare festivals, and major conservatory training programs. Although I lacked experience in running a theatre of ASF's size and scale, the combination of my theatrical experience and my Southern heritage aligned with the needs and preferences of the company (i.e., Shakespeare and classics, an MFA training program, and the South's love of language, well-told stories, and writers). Most of all, I was onsite during the search process. *On the Verge* opened in the spring, and by mid-July I had been hired as artistic director, aided by recommendations of my two mentors, Michael Langham and Mark Lamos. The timing was definitely on my side;
- **Most important!** To have the best chance of being interviewed and considered seriously for many artistic director jobs, you will need to have nurtured prior, positive relationships with the leading "Search

Consultants" in the field. They should be aware of you and your work long before the job becomes open. Your communication and networking plan should include reaching out to these search consultants. These "Recruiters" are widely connected in the theatre (and the performing arts) field, and have tremendous influence when hired to manage a search. Direct contacts or recommendations by your mentors, advocates, industry leaders, and artistic directors will also open doors to these "search firms." Again, begin the relationship long before the jobs open up.

If you decide to pursue an opening for an artistic director, read on. The next chapter covers the typical search, interview, and hiring process that most theatres follow in hiring a new artistic director.

12

Getting the
Artistic Director Job

Typical search process

Boards of Trustees recognize that the selection of a new artistic leader is one of the most important decisions they will make for the theatre. During the process, trustees often learn a lot about the theatre field, their organization, and its potential. They will hear many different and compelling visions for the organization's future and interview several candidates. The search for a new leader usually takes several months. For most mid-size to larger theatres, Boards follow similar steps in the hiring of new artistic leadership. Until late in the process, the search is kept confidential to protect the privacy of the theatre's deliberations and of any candidates who currently hold leadership positions at other institutions. All candidates are expected to honor that confidentiality. Here's an overview of the process:

1 The Chair appoints a Search Committee of the Board, which may or may not include the managing director, senior staff members, major philanthropists, and community leaders.

2 The search committee interviews and then hires a professional recruiter (or search consultant) to handle the search. Some Boards may choose to undertake the search process themselves, but most wisely hire a specialist who has widespread knowledge of the theatre field.

3 The recruiter interviews several trustees, including the chair and the search committee as well as select senior staff. Then he takes what he's learned and creates a "Candidate Briefing" (UK) or "Job Profile" (US). As the Job Profile is being completed and posted, the recruiter is simultaneously reaching out to field leaders and colleagues for their recommendations. He may also reach out to highly qualified and accomplished individuals whom he believes would make exceptional candidates, hoping to persuade them to apply.

4 After incorporating any revisions requested by the search committee, the Job Profile is published and posted online, on the theatre's and the search consultant's websites. This is the moment the search goes "live."

5 As applications arrive, the recruiter reviews them and contacts anyone who catches his interest. In addition, he will contact and interview any candidate requested by the search committee, including current staff members, prior guest directors, and local theatre artists.

6 Once the announced deadline for applications has passed, the recruiter reviews his notes and the candidates' paperwork. He then narrows down the list of names and **confidentially** checks each candidate's accomplishments and reputation within the field.

7 At a pre-arranged date, the recruiter meets with the search committee to present his top recommendations. He includes each candidate's paperwork, but also discusses the background and experience, providing his reasoning for including the person. Frequently, the list of recommended candidates includes three levels of candidates: (1) deeply experienced, successful artistic leaders who could easily step into the job; (2) moderately experienced, promising candidates whom the recruiter believes are ready and eager to step up into the role of artistic director (e,g., artistic directors at smaller theatres or resident

directors at similar institutions); and (3) "high risk/high reward" candidates who are exceptionally gifted, dynamic, and visionary artists, but lack experience as organizational leaders. After discussion with the recruiter, the search committee reduces the list for initial interviews.

8 Best field practices in recruiting an artistic director include at least two onsite interviews with the full search committee. However, this depends upon the resources and location of the theatre. Current practice includes three interviews: Preliminary, Shortlist, and Final. A subset of the search committee may hold Preliminary Interviews via video conference or phone with each candidate, which typically lasts for an hour or so. After the Preliminary Interviews are completed, the search committee (with assistance from the recruiter) reduces the list of candidates again to "The Shortlist."

9 The search committee then meets in person with each candidate on The Shortlist. Once this round of interviews is completed, the search committee will discuss each candidate at length. They may ask the recruiter for additional information on specific candidates. After all of the information is reviewed, the committee reduces the list to a handful of finalists who are notified. Note: **This point generally marks the end of strict confidentiality**. Prior to the Final Interviews, the search committee, the chair, and the recruiter call the list of references submitted by each candidate. Many widen the net, calling business colleagues or fellow trustees they know around the country who may be aware of a finalist's working style, reputation, and accomplishments. Typically, this is the time when candidates who currently head other organizations inform the leadership of their Board, the managing director, and select members of their artistic staff.

10 The schedule for the Final Interview is intense and often jam-packed. Over the course of one day and evening, each finalist will meet with the search committee, the chair, the senior staff, artistic and production leaders, major donors, significant community partners or leaders, and perhaps small groups of employees from many departments. The day often includes a reception with the full Board and their spouses/ partners to observe your interpersonal skills and speaking talents in a larger, social setting. If there is a show running, the evening may also include seeing a performance.

11 Following the Final Interviews, the search committee ranks the candidates in order of preference, votes and makes a recommendation

to the chair (or perhaps to the full Board). Once approved, the first choice receives an offer and negotiations begin.

Initial contacts

There are three kinds of initial contacts with a recruiter (or search committee chair), including:

1 **Least frequent:** She contacts you based upon her review of your self-submitted application and paperwork.
2 **More frequent:** She contacts you based upon professional recommendations.
3 **Most frequent:** She contacts you, because she knows your work and you (and often has professional recommendations).

In (1) and (2), the recruiter will briefly describe the theatre, its challenges and opportunities, and the type of leader the Board is seeking. However, the bulk of the time will be spent "getting to know you," asking questions about your background, experience, etc., and finding out about your qualifications for the job. This is more **interview than conversation**. Although this contact may not lead to pursuing you for the job in question, it provides an excellent opportunity to meet the recruiter and make her more aware of your work and you.

In (3), the recruiter will cover the same information, but answer your questions in greater detail, ask about your interest in the position, and encourage you to apply. This is more **conversation than interview**.

The job profile

With or **without** contact from the recruiter, to create the best application, you must find and review the Job Profile. These are often found online at the theatre's website, and on public and paid job-listing sites online or in the press. For the purposes of this section, I researched several current listings and created a profile for "Theatre MNO"—a fictitious organization. (I will note that language in this typeface.) Job Profiles may include the following:

• **Brief History of the Organization**, noting the theatre's significance in the national, regional and/or local theatre scene. It also describes the theatre's signature achievements and successes and its impact on the community.

- **Information on the City and Region** where the theatre is located. Often this is "promotional" information created by the local government or civic/business groups to attract executives and businesses to the region.
- Names and Bios of **Current Leadership**. This or another section will include a history of the prior artistic director, the planned date for his departure, and **any changes in organizational structure**.
- **Opportunities and Challenges** lists current promising developments (e.g., renewal of the surrounding inner city, growth in millennial population, new programming initiatives, etc.) and difficulties facing the organization (e.g., programming no longer relevant, declining subscriptions, need for increased contributed or subsidized revenue, competition for patrons from other cultural or entertainment offerings, and more). Look for critical information in this section, such as "the Board and organization faces the first artistic leadership transition in two decades and recognizes its increased need to support the new artistic director, both in governance and in fundraising."
- **Current Environment** or **Operations** includes the number of shows produced or presented, titles, number of theatre spaces, and an overview of the performance calendar. This often includes the annual number of tickets sold, the number of subscribers, the annual operating budget, any special funds or endowments, the size of full-time, seasonal staff and guest artists, and relevant union agreements. This section may also list additional signature programs, such as a New Play or Musical program, Conservatory Training, Arts in Education, Community Engagement, etc.
- **Position and Responsibilities** lays out the **Artistic** and **the Institutional duties of the job.**
  Theatre MNO's profile states:
  Artistic Leadership. The artistic director will be expected:
  - to be the company's artistic guide in choosing plays and other programs it will present, in ways that recognize Theatre MNO's distinguished history and its interest in making theatre even more relevant to today's audiences; to choose creative teams for the productions; and to assure high standards of excellence;
  - to establish and maintain strong relationships with upcoming and established playwrights, directors, actors, and designers, to keep Theatre MNO at the forefront of American regional theatre;

- to broaden Theatre MNO's impact in the United States and abroad, through co-productions, joint commissions, transfers, and by all other appropriate means;
- to make choices in content and performance that attract an audience that looks like the increasingly diverse and young population of our region;
- to work closely with the Education and Community Engagement leaders to expand the visibility of those programs and the communities they serve;
- to assist in forming and maintaining authentic and lasting relationships in diverse communities so that Theatre MNO remains an institution that matters in its region;
- to consider all ways that will energize ever larger audiences to take part in the many aspects of the theatre's work.

Organizational Leadership. The artistic director will be expected:

- to be a deeply committed organizational leader of the artistic and administrative staff, managing the positions that report to the artistic director and setting a culture of respect and collaboration;
- to be a leader and resource to the Board of Trustees, assuring that these volunteers have the information and motivation to function effectively;
- to embody Theatre MNO's mission and values, and to inspire others to do the same, continuing the theatre's efforts to create a more diverse organization on its stages, in its communities, and its staff, artists, Board, and audiences, enhancing Theatre MNO's position as a good public citizen of the region;
- to develop a vision for the theatre that recognizes the importance of its mission, and excites its artists, Board, and staff;
- to serve as the public face and spokesperson of the institution, including taking part in selective cultivation of major donors;
- to help develop the resources to energize ever larger audiences, to make Theatre MNO one of the most diverse theatres in America, and to clearly establish it as one of the major theatre companies in the country.

- **Qualifications** is often presented as a long (and daunting) list of the professional experience, demonstrated achievement, reputation, artistry, and leadership required for a candidate to be strongly considered. To be fair, these sections often state, "No one person will fully meet all these qualifications."

Theatre MNO's **Qualifications** include:

- o demonstrated capacity to articulate a strong aesthetic and overall vision that inspires others;
- o a known breadth of interests to explore a full range of theatre in both a national and international context, including a role in the world of new play development;
- o a proven leader who demonstrates a grasp of how artistic choice and the operational, financial, and producing elements of the theatre must work together;
- o while the Committee will not exclude other candidates, there is a bias towards someone who has demonstrated artistic achievement in the theatre world;
- o prior experience in an organizational leadership role or at least oversight of important projects will be preferred, but not absolutely required.

- **Personal Values, Traits or Qualities**:
  - o delight at the prospect of fulfilling the theatre's mission and values; this includes a demonstrable belief in Community Engagement and Arts Education, as well as in professional theatre producing;
  - o a proven commitment to equity, diversity, and inclusion that the candidate has demonstrated within professional work or leadership;
  - o a desire to engage with a variety of the region's communities and a lively curiosity about people and their concerns;
  - o the interest and the capability to build relationships with major donors and community leaders.

- **Salary and Benefits** are often described in general terms, such as "salary and benefits package will be competitive with other companies of comparable stature and size." Some theatres will ask you to include your salary history and requirements.

- **Application Instructions** tells "**interested**" and "**qualified**" candidates how to apply, including the required paperwork and how to submit the application.

- **Commitments to Diverse and Female Candidates.** In the US, many theatres will state, "We encourage applications from women and from persons of color." Certain theatres are now embracing more sophisticated and expansive statements such as "The Guthrie is dedicated to building a culturally diverse and equitable environment and strongly encourages applications from people of color and women.

This position will remain open until filled and until a diverse and qualified pool of candidates is identified. Applicants from populations underrepresented in the theatre field are strongly encouraged to apply." In the UK, part of the application process includes filling out an "Equal Opportunity Monitoring Form."

Evaluating the job profile

After reading it a few times, ask yourself several questions: How well do you and your work meet the necessary requirements of the job? If you meet only a few of the requirements, don't apply. If you meet several of the requirements, what specific strengths, talent, and experiences can you bring to the position? What is most exciting about the post? What is least exciting? What questions would you have for the recruiter? If interviewed, what comments and questions would you have for the Board, the managing director, or senior staff?

Looking at the quotes from Theatre MNO's profile, I surmise that the Board believes the current artistic director selected shows based upon his personal aesthetic without adequate consideration of audience interest, financial, and labor impact on the rest of the organization and the communities being served. They clearly desire someone who will balance the resources and opportunities of its other major programs (i.e., Arts Education and Community Engagement) with those of the mainstage productions. Jot down questions. Does the Board believe too much (or too little) is spent on mainstage or on the other two areas? It also appears that Theatre MNO wants a strong fundraiser, a leader who can engage many diverse communities, the local theatre community, and other major cultural organizations of the region. It's seeking a dynamic, well-connected, high achieving, visionary, and **collaborative** artistic leader.

In every Job Profile, look for warning signs, such as repetition or contradictory and conflicting expectations of the new artistic director. For me, one warning sign in the above profile is its description of the first artistic responsibility: "To be the company's artistic guide in choosing plays and other programs it will present." Traditionally, an artistic director's fundamental responsibility and authority is to select the season and any artistic programs. What does the theatre mean by "artistic guide"? Does it mean that seasons will be chosen by a group of leaders? Or does it simply reflect a need for conversation and consultation with the managing director during the process of season selection?

Repetition can be the result of a document written by committee, but it also may reflect the high importance of a requirement or expectation in the next leader. Repeated criteria calling for effective, careful, or disciplined use of resources may reveal your predecessor's stubborn refusal to even consider the financial and human consequences of his programming choices. In small to mid-size organizations, the profile may list several full-time jobs for the position (e.g., artistic director, lead fundraiser, institutional leader, frequent director, faculty member, and/or impassioned seeker of pre-Broadway shows). Another theatre may state that they are looking for a brilliantly innovative and imaginative artistic director who is preferably diverse and/or female, but later state that candidates must have 10–15+ years of experience leading a large institution. The former is admirable but disingenuous when the latter automatically eliminates many female and/or diverse candidates. Another theatre might seek to hire a nationally acclaimed director of world premieres, but also require her "mitigate risk" by selecting shows that will meet "income and attendance projections." By their nature, world premieres are artistic and financial risks. Furthermore, believing that an artistic director can always pick "winners" is absurd and reflects a Board's lack of understanding of the art form. There are other clues, too. Other criteria may ask for new and imaginative programming, because the current shows are dated and not attracting audiences of a sufficient size to sustain the theatre. Indeed, by careful reading you can often sense a Board's frustration or dissatisfaction with your predecessor. As with script analysis, you must "read between the lines" to find the meaning. Jot down questions and topics for discussion with the recruiter or the search committee.

Many profiles are extensive and complete, with links to documents, and production photos. If any information is missing, the recruiter may be able to help you, but be proactive in finding it yourself. Make a point of being informed about the theatre, its mission and vision, history, and the community it serves. This information will make your application more effective.

Your application

When applying, follow the instructions **precisely**. Provide the required paperwork (typically a cover letter, resumé [US] or CV [UK], and a list of professional references or letters of recommendation). Check the deadline and beat it. Follow the steps to submit the application—often online. In addition, there are often directives, such as "covering letter should outline your vision for the future of the artistic programme" or "the letter should not exceed two pages." Follow them. If there are no directives regarding the letter's content, you should communicate why this post and theatre is especially attractive to you and what it is about you and your work that would make you a strong and competitive candidate for its next artistic director. Make sure to communicate your passion for the job and to describe some of the artistic opportunities you see or perceive for the theatre—these ideas are the beginning steps in creating your artistic vision. Acknowledge the past achievements and accomplishments of the theatre and your predecessor. If you need help with writing or editing, ask a friend who's an accomplished writer to assist you. Keep your letter to a couple of pages. Review your resumé for its relevance to the job and trim as necessary. Unless the profile specifically requests additional materials (e.g., production photos, reviews, etc.), don't include them. If you are asked to submit a list of references, contact each person to ask permission and for the best way for the recruiter to contact them. If you need letters of recommendation, contact the individuals well in advance of the deadline.

The interviews

A respected recruiter writes, "In any search, I encourage candidates to make two lists:

- First, what do you want the Search Committee to know about you that meets the criteria outlined in the Job Profile?
- Second, what do you want/need to know about the Board, staff, or organization? That is, what information stands between your receiving an offer and accepting it? Failing to explore critical issues or significant problems during the interviews often has unhappy consequences (in a generally not-too-distant future) after you've taken the job."

When you are invited to a Preliminary Interview, the recruiter typically contacts you with specific information based upon his presentation of your application to the search committee. Prepare answers for any specific concerns by the committee. Recruiters often send the names of committee members who will be interviewing you; if so, look up their bios online. During a Preliminary Interview, time is short (remember that the committee is talking with multiple candidates), so focus on the key points you want them to know, such as your high interest in the theatre, how you meet the criteria, and how you will advance the institution. You'll likely be asked several questions such as: What's your personal and professional history? What do you think about the current programming? What can you bring as a leader? Then the committee may ask you specific questions about your resumé, your leadership style and the working culture you would create, your artistic vision and preferences, past fundraising experience, interaction with Boards, partnerships with managing directors, experience in supporting diversity and inclusion, and more. Answer the questions you're asked with candor, but also share your excitement and passion for the position. Always approach the interviews and meetings as a positive opportunity for you as an artist and leader. At the end, you may have time for additional comments and questions. Take a moment to check the list of the issues you wanted to address with the search committee and ask questions for clarification. Be aware that the later, onsite interviews are a better time to address substantive issues. After the conversation, note your reactions to the information you heard and your impression of the trustees with whom you spoke. Note any questions or topics you could address better in the future interviews. Write down any additional reasons you want to apply, as well as any concerns or red flags that emerged during the interview.

Note: **If you decide that you don't want the job, let the search consultant know immediately.** It's neither professional nor considerate to ask a theatre to continue a time-consuming and expensive process, if you have already decided that you won't take the job.

Replacing a Founder or a Long-time Leader

Following a founder or "venerated" multi-year artistic director can be tricky. If your predecessor is on the search committee, that's a red flag. Observe the influence he wields. Another red flag is when the theatre has made future contractual commitments to your predecessor. Effectively this means you will be "leading" in the shadow of the prior artistic director. No theatre should expect a new artistic director to be obligated in any way to his predecessor, no matter the length of his tenure or success. There are many cautionary tales of artistic or managing directors who followed long-term leaders and ended up as "transitional leaders." Unfortunately, these leaders were doomed to become "the transition" between a revered, long-term leader and a truly empowered, future leader. Another potentially complicated situation is being the favorite candidate of the departing artistic director. This can be a double-edged sword. It can be an advantage or a liability for your candidacy. The best way to handle such a situation is to go through the application and interview process professionally without help from the prior leader.

The shortlist

You've made it to the Shortlist. Congratulations! The search committee has decided that you are a strong candidate and wants to interview you in person. To prepare for an onsite interview, review your submitted materials, the notes from the Preliminary Interview, and ask the recruiter for feedback on it (e.g., what can I improve?), and ask for any counsel moving forward. Give some thought to your earlier answers and revise as necessary. Do some additional research on the community, including its demographics and diversity, its economic condition, and whatever else you find attractive about the area. Look up bios for the artistic and production leaders, and the senior staff of the theatre. If you haven't received Financial Statements, Budgets, or Audits (US) or Annual Reviews (UK), ask for them immediately. When a theatre refuses or avoids sharing its financial information with candidates, it often indicates substantial financial problems. If you need help understanding these spreadsheets or reports, ask a friend who has a financial background. Review any upcoming professional or personal commitments you have (e.g., directing a show, your wedding, etc.). Mention that you have these conflicts during the interview.

At this interview, you are promoting yourself as the most exciting choice for artistic director, but be aware that the Board is also evaluating your potential as a future organizational leader. After your initial presentation or round of questions, treat the interview as a conversation—a give-and-take between professionals who love the art form. Answer the questions in a straightforward manner. Give the committee an overview of your artistic vision for the organization. Introduce your larger ideas and proposed changes, such as producing more plays by women playwrights, pursuing a more diverse lineup of titles, creating theatre for a new generation of audiences or a specific underserved audience, or developing new musicals with commercial producers. If you've done your research well, you can link your ideas to the production history (e.g., out of 250+ mainstage productions, less than a dozen have been written by women and only seven were directed by women). If approximately 14 percent of the population of metropolitan London are Muslim, how do you plan to shift programming and/or community engagement to serve that community? How do you want to change the organization? If you want to make major changes in programming, staffing, and more, lay the groundwork for this. Above all, be straightforward and positive. The search committee should also be "promoting" the job and theatre and courting your interest. After all, you've made the Shortlist, and they hope and want to find a future leader—perhaps you. At the same time, you are deciding whether this theatre continues to interest you or not.

In-person interviews are a great time to evaluate the commitment of the chair and the search committee to the theatre and its programs. Do they love and admire the productions and artistic initiatives? What titles, genres, or types of theatre most engage them? Are they focused on mainstage shows or other programs and activities (e.g., arts in education, student matinees, or "taking shows to Broadway")? Are they knowledgeable about the theatre field? Do they appreciate and admire the people who work in theatre? Do they understand the language of subsidized/not-for-profit theatre and the performing arts? Do they regard the theatre as vital to the quality of life in their city? Are they solely concerned with the bottom line? Do they speak in the language of the business world? Sometimes trustees only seem to know and understand the corporate language that they use in their careers. Dig a little deeper. A terrific tool to uncover individual appreciation and passion about the theatre's work is to ask each board member to tell you what performance, event, or moment has been most memorable and meaningful to them at the theatre. The answers are often surprising, because each person will identify different productions or programs, often with delight, emotion, and insight.

The interviews may include a personal meeting with the managing director. This is a good opportunity to talk with the person who will be your future partner. Have a conversation with her about the current state of the organization, what kind of partnership she would want to build, and what she hopes the new artistic director will bring to the theatre. Ask what her biggest challenges are. This is also a good moment to ask for details about ticket sales, including percentage of capacity sold across recent seasons (that is, of all seats available for sale, what percentage were sold?). Also, ask for her favorite performances, events, or programs. Evaluate how much she loves the art form. Also, mention any commitments or conflicts to her that you have upcoming.

After the first onsite interview, follow the same process of review and note-taking as before, but focus on what most excites you about the job and theatre as well as what worries or concerns you. Evaluate your performance in the interview.

The final interview

You've make it to the Final Interviews. Congratulations! You are one of very few candidates selected and your odds of getting the job have improved enormously. To prepare, review all your notes and talk with the recruiter for feedback and counsel. Then spend time refining and improving your artistic vision and plans for change at the theatre. Acknowledge and express your appreciation for the past work of the theatre and its current artistic director, but focus on the future. Of course, your vision remains a "work in progress," which you should not forget to mention. Because Final Interviews are often non-stop and you will be meeting many more people, craft **talking points in advance** that include: your excitement about the job and theatre, your artistic vision, and some key initiatives or changes you want to focus on in the near term. You will be repeating these talking points many times during the day and evening. In addition, make a list of your **key concerns** that you need to be addressed by the end of the day. As you know from freelance directing, every theatre has its problems and challenges as well as its successes and strengths; therefore, focus only on the most important issues of concern.

Often the day will begin with a breakfast with the chair, members of the search committee, or the managing director; this is followed by a lengthy meeting with the full search committee. At this Final Interview, review your artistic vision for the theatre, but also lay out your top priorities if you're offered the job, including any new programs and artistic advancements, as well as possible changes in staffing or operations. Laying out your biggest ideas and plans also reminds the trustees of the additional resources your vision will require. Remember that every meal will be a working meal. Prepare to talk a lot and answer a lot of questions. Get the rest and the food you need during the days leading up to the interview, and make your travel plans so that you can arrive in good time the day before the interview.

A Final Interview day and evening gives you time to evaluate the theatre's overall commitment and capacity to change. The trustees and staff may profess their desire for change, but find out what that means. The desire and support for change may be genuine, but sometimes the Board and the company want you to respect the status quo and only make specific, smaller changes that each has long wanted. This day often reveals the working culture of the organization, including any fixation on "that's the way we've always done it," entrenched behavior, the overall approach to success and failure, and the engagement of Trustees under the prior AD.

You will likely meet with the managing director, the artistic staff, the production manager, the senior staff, the artistic staff and perhaps small groups of employees from across the organization. Before meeting with staff and company members, remind yourself of who is interviewing whom. Many staff and company members are understandably anxious about their job security in the future, and they may ask inappropriate or challenging questions; don't answer them, instead take note of the underlying tensions behind those questions. Share your enthusiasm for the job and high-level ideas, but also get the information you need to know from the staff. Ask questions to evaluate their overall commitment to the theatre and their excitement about a new artistic leader.

The results

If you get the job, celebrate! Briefly. You will immediately begin contractual negotiations. Many of us choose to hire an attorney experienced in theatrical employment to undertake this process. The agreement must be put into writing by the theatre. It should include a list of authorities, responsibilities and duties as artistic director, the reporting and organizational structure, your compensation and benefits, length of contract, and any other relevant terms of employment. Put in writing your upcoming professional or personal commitments. Establish the maximum number of shows that you will direct each season for the theatre, after which you should earn additional compensation. This provides an important protection for you that can keep you more effective in your "day job"—artistic direction. If you end up directing too many shows to reduce expenses, you run the risk of exhaustion and burnout. Stipulate in your contract if you want the opportunity to direct elsewhere and solicit the recruiter's help in informing the Board of the mutual benefits of doing so for both you and the theatre.

For artistic and managing directors, the industry's best practice is offering multi-year appointments. These provide assurance and commitment from both sides and ensure a continuous relationship over multiple seasons. In addition, they prevent your performance (and employment) from being judged on a single production or part of a single season. Finally, if there is a significant gap between your offer and the beginning of full-time employment, the contract should stipulate how much you are paid (often as a fee) for work prior to you assuming the job full time. Carefully review your schedule between now and your start date to include your personal needs— moving, travel, meeting, staff support, etc.

If this process doesn't land you a job, don't despair. Ask the search consultant for comments or tips for improvement for each part of the interview process. Write down your own thoughts about the process, noting what you did well and what you did not. Don't be too self-critical; remain balanced and positive. Interviewing for these jobs takes practice. Your confidence, skill, and success rate will improve dramatically when you have been through the search process a few times.

13

Preparing to Lead

Congratulations again on your appointment as artistic director! You've achieved a major career goal and now you have an important and significant chance to lead the theatre to new heights of artistic achievement and organizational success. When your contract is finalized and signed, the pace will accelerate and you will face multiple tasks, many of which must be addressed at the same time.

Announcing your appointment

If you are currently employed at another theatre or organization, you need to give official notice to your Board Chair or boss. Although you have already informed a handful of staff and board members prior to the Final Interviews, you will want to inform your colleagues and company members, the rest of the trustees, and important donors and supporters as soon as possible. At the same time, the new theatre's marketing and PR department will be preparing a press release/media announcement, which will include your bio and quotes from you. Once you give your notice, they will hopefully reach out to your current organization to coordinate announcements. In the best of worlds, the releases will be distributed to significant press/media partners in advance but embargoed until a formal press event—either a press conference or, more commonly, a series of interviews with media writers. In your quotes and interviews, express your passion and excitement at becoming the next artistic director, briefly praise the work of the theatre and your predecessor, and give an overview of your top priorities. Share the major ideas you will be pursuing, and the reasoning behind them as well as how you hope to accomplish them. Don't overshare your plans. While it's important to express your vision and ideas for the future, you also need time to **find out what you don't know** before you declare specific goals and timelines. For instance, if you want to create a new play program and festival, say so and why, but frame it as a multi-season project. If you want to produce more plays by playwrights of a specific diversity (e.g., East Asian communities of London), say so and explain why, but avoid going into details. This is not to be disingenuous; rather, it gives you the time to create a plan that can be accomplished, including what the organization needs to do to make your ideas happen. This seemingly cautious approach also prevents you from promising something you cannot deliver. Again, hopefully, on the same day as the formal press event, you will be introduced to the entire staff and company and be given time to present your plans and aspirations at each gathering. Most will include a question-and-answer session. Depending upon the schedule, the theatre may hold a social occasion or meal with the entire Board and senior staff.

Understanding the transition

The same skill set you learned to manage your time, focus, and energy in juggling a freelance career will serve you well during the transition period as the incoming artistic director. In many cases, an artistic director announces his departure at the end of the current or next season. Most Boards endeavor to appoint a new artistic leader well in advance of the departure of the previous artistic director, intending a period of overlap. If you are onsite before your predecessor departs, ask to meet with him. Interview him, ask about his experiences and practices, the good times and the tough times in the job, etc. Although you may not end up agreeing, ask for his advice and perspective on the theatre. Always treat your predecessor with respect. His work and achievements have made it possible for you to be hired.

If your full-time appointment doesn't begin for several months, your first task will be to work out, based on your signed contract, the dates and times you can work on behalf of the theatre, both onsite and offsite. Review the immediate tasks you need to address. For example, when I was hired at the Denver Center, I was told I had only six weeks to pick the next season. Continuing to lead the Alabama Shakespeare Festival, I missed that deadline, but not by much. Your discussions with the Board and the managing director during negotiations should have included a list of any urgent tasks and deadlines. In your scheduling, remember to include your own professional and personal commitments (including directing productions elsewhere, organizing your move, making temporary housing arrangements, selling or buying a home, finding schools, etc.). Focus on the most essential tasks you need to accomplish before starting full-time.

Take control of your calendar

Ask for a point person on the staff (often the current artistic or managing director's assistant) to handle your calendar and all requests for your time. Meet the assistant. Talk about how you'd like to handle meeting requests, correspondence, email, messages, etc. Ask him to widely distribute the dates and times that you will be onsite, and to block out dates of personal and professional conflicts. Ask the artistic, production, and management staffs to help the assistant put together a notebook with relevant and important information, including production calendars, contact sheets for the Board and staff, current budgets and sales reports, etc., regular internal meetings, galas or annual events, Board and Committee meetings.

Build relationships

- **Meet and/or talk frequently with your partner, the managing director.** This is your most important task. Establish regular times to meet or check in. Learn from her how the organization operates, how it budgets, the typical schedule for season selection, etc. In her opinion, what are the most important issues that need your immediate attention? Share your vision and your ideas for advancing the theatre and listen to her feedback, ideas, and concerns. Describe the working relationship you want to develop with her and listen to her thoughts. It is vital to engage her in your future vision and aspirations. Ask her to evaluate the strengths and weaknesses of Board, staff, artists, etc. Be straightforward but stay persuasive and positive. Commit to the relationship.

- **Stay connected with the Trustees.** Trustees will often hold dinners or receptions in your honor to introduce you socially to fellow trustees, significant donors and local leaders. After this initial round of social occasions, trustees may drift away. This makes sense. After hiring you, the chair and the search committee are often fatigued, given the long hours, hard decisions, and energy they've devoted to the Search Process. Recruiters remind them that you (as the new leader) will need their active support, counsel, and presence in your first year. The chair or members of the search committee may be active in keeping in touch with you, but don't take it for granted, as they can sometimes seem to vanish. Take proactive responsibility: talk to the chair regularly, and arrange to meet with all of the trustees either individually or in small groups during your first season. Your managing director and the development director can help guide you in setting up these meetings. Along with the marketing director, they can also introduce you to significant partners, donors, government officials, and community leaders as well as set up speaking engagements.
- **Meet the senior staff.** Although most theatres will hold a companywide reception for the incoming artistic director, take the time to meet with each member of the senior staff or leadership team.
- **Meet the artistic and literary staff.** Spend time with them discussing how they approach their work, how the various duties and responsibilities are divided up, and learn their personal artistic passions and interests. Ask them for their schedules and to identify upcoming decision points. Find out which national theatre conferences, new play or musical festivals, etc., the prior artistic director or they attended.
- **Meet the production manager and department heads.** Spend time reviewing the entire production process from season selection through closing night from their perspective.
- Once onsite, schedule meetings with **any remaining leaders on staff** and **significant supporters**, including:

- ○ **Management leaders,** including the **directors of:**
  - ▪ **Marketing/PR/communications**. Also, the house management and box office staff as they have the closest contact with audiences.
  - ▪ **Development or advancement.** Get to know the current sources of support or subsidy, and share your ideas for new fundraising opportunities based upon your vision and goals.
  - ▪ **Finance and accounting.** Ask for their assistance in understanding financial reports, such as sales reports, budgets, and audits.
- ○ **Volunteers.**
- ○ **External stakeholders.** Ask the managing director and the development and marketing directors to create a prioritized list of the external stakeholders you should meet over the first season, including:
  - ▪ Important partners (e.g., an umbrella organization that operates the facilities);
  - ▪ Major donors and foundations;
  - ▪ Government officials or agencies (e.g., the Arts Council);
  - ▪ Regional and national funders and foundations;
  - ▪ Community leaders;
  - ▪ Local theatre companies. Rely upon the artistic staff to provide information about the local theatre community, including other organizations, leaders, and professional artists;
  - ▪ When you have the time and opportunity, meet or talk with regular guest artists (local or out-of-town) who interest you.

Learn what you don't know

A vitally important task is understanding the resources (both human and financial) available to produce the shows and operate the theatre. Be persistent in this—press further—you need to fully comprehend what those resources can accomplish. For instance, every production staff member has a level of experience, talent, and expertise which can make a modest budget go very far ... or not. During your first couple of seasons you will begin to comprehend the variables of money, staff, and talent available to you, as well as the local cost of materials, and the necessary build times, etc. If you've directed at the theatre or seen several shows there, this process will be quicker. Spend time with your production manager discussing these issues.

This will inform your decisions on season selection, designers, fees, the allocating of resources, etc., but take care not to let this knowledge dampen your artistic vision. Though you may have more day-to-day interaction with them, be aware that production managers often report to the managing director on fiscal and operational matters. This leads some production managers to undercommit resources (or say "no") so that they never exceed their budgets or press their staffs. Having a three-way conversation with the managing director, the production manager and you can be very useful at the beginning of your tenure.

Putting your vision into action

Achieving your artistic vision is a stimulating but often complicated task. You should know that every artistic director has a "honeymoon period" with trustees and funders, who are naturally excited about your arrival as the new leader and stimulated by your ideas and vision. Take advantage of this time; ask for what you will need to achieve your vision **that is above and beyond the normal funding needed for the annual operating budget**.

- **Decide on your top priorities.** Make a list of everything (large and small) that you hope to create, change, improve, and accomplish as an artistic director and organizational leader. For example, your list may include hiring a new production manager, changing the resident acting company, starting a new play program, finding a new assistant, hiring an associate artistic director, or radically changing the programmatic mix. That's ambitious but what's the most important to you? Be ruthless in prioritizing your list. Your choices should demonstrate your vision and reflect your leadership style. This list may change as you observe the theatre in action and work with the staff. In the beginning, most of us are very excited by the many opportunities and challenges of the job, and we want to address, fix or improve as much as we can. Pragmatically, you can only accomplish a handful of changes in the first year. In your first season, force yourself to focus on the top 3–5 changes that are most important and most feasible. *Don't pick more!* Having 10–15 changes will fragment your focus, frustrate you, and unsettle the staff; and a long list of changes can easily imply that you are dissatisfied with everyone and everything. In selecting your 3–5 priorities, pick one or two that are easy fixes or changes, and pick a couple that are big ideas that will boldly advance the artistic work. Enlist the help and experienced leadership of the managing director in accomplishing these changes. If the changes are major (e.g., eliminating the resident acting company), keep the Board leadership informed of your intentions and your timeline, so they are prepared to support you.

- **Hiring and firing.** There are often excellent reasons for not renewing or terminating the contracts of current staff and resident company members and/or artists. You may want to, and should, bring in your own staff and artists. A specific staff member may have proven a disruptive person who was tolerated by your predecessor. Long-time employees may have become entitled or ineffective. You may want to diversify your staff and company. There are two extreme approaches of hiring and firing staff and company by incoming artistic directors. On one extreme, artistic directors "wipe the slate clean" by letting go of all staff and company. In my mind, this extreme is unwise unless **absolutely necessary for institutional survival**. If you don't handle it well, you will be perceived as brutal, arrogant, or autocratic. If you plan to make such a sweeping change, you should have discussed it during your interviews, and followed up repeatedly with your managing director and the Board leadership. However, the most significant reason I advise against this course of action is the consequent loss of organizational knowledge and commitment. The other extreme is when an artistic director keeps everyone employed. This is equally unwise as it implies that there will be no changes in personnel, working culture, artistic focus, operating methods, or expectations. This can lead to significant resistance and upset when you begin making changes. You will often find more success by adopting a middle path. You should establish your own artistic and production team, hire the artists with whom you want to work, and lead the theatre in a new direction, but this is often best achieved through a combination of new and current employees and artists. If time permits, there is another approach in which you set a period to watch the staff and regular artists in action, and then make a decision at a logical moment in time (e.g., the end of the season). Although it can be unsettling to the organization, it's far better to talk about the timeframe for change in advance. Handle the personnel changes thoughtfully and professionally. Talk with the individuals who are leaving and (if possible) give them adequate advance notice so they can find other work.

Selling your vision

Many aspirants to artistic direction believe the core job is leading by ordering, directing or demanding results from the staff, the company, the artists, and even the Board. There is some measure of truth in this—a strong leader must set the vision, goals, and expectations of the theatre and hold everyone accountable. However, the core job more often is leading by persuading, inspiring, asking, and cultivating allies. You will need a lot of support from advocates, donors, staff, and leaders. You must attract and lead many different people towards a new and better future. This will take an enormous amount of time and a lot of personal interaction with many different stakeholders. As you continuously refine and improve your vision and goals, craft several "Elevator Speeches" and "Bulleted Talking Points" for the many different people and groups that you will meet and want to engage as collaborators.

Leading and Managing Change

As the new artistic director, you are expected to renew, reinvent or reimagine the artistic vision of the theatre. You and the managing director will be effecting and managing change throughout the organization to achieve your artistic vision. The most common behaviors during a significant change in a business organization are illustrated by the "bell curve of change." This concept is based upon multiple published studies. The bell curve of change indicates that 15 percent of people will actively resist the change ("over my dead body"), 35 percent will be disinclined or dislike it, 35 percent will like the idea but wait for additional proof, and 15 percent will be enthusiastic supporters and advocates (i.e., early adopters). As the instigator of change, engage and nurture the early adopters of your artistic vision first. These early adopters tend to be spread up and down the organizational structure. They will be fans, advocates, and in some cases "change leaders." They can often persuade the 35 percent who are inclined but hesitant as well as influence others. Several business consultants suggest a leader must also have "mental toughness." If you believe the change is necessary and important, stay true to your decision. As you identify the 15 percent who are opposed to any change, you and the managing director will need to determine an exit plan for them.

An unpleasant surprise

Most artistic directors learn something troubling, surprising, or unsettling about the theatre that they were not told during the interviews. When it's financial instability, it's likely that you were purposely not told **and** that you didn't ask the necessary questions during the interview. If several important staff members leave suddenly within days of your announcement, it's probably not you, but something that you were not told; it's likely someone knew but declined to inform you. Unless it's institution-threatening or seriously undermines your ability to lead, take it in stride. As one of my mentors told me, "Welcome to the Field!" Discuss these issues with your managing director, the Board chair, the executive committee (if appropriate), and the relevant staff. Work towards solving the issue, but also talk with whoever declined to disclose the information; tell her that you expect disclosure and transparency in the future. If it truly is institution-threatening or likely damaging to your success, contact the Search Consultant immediately.

Final thoughts

Artistic directing can be the most exciting time in your professional career. You will hear from dozens of people, many congratulating you and praising your appointment. Many are genuine, but many also want you to hire them. Enjoy the congratulations but ignore the flattery. While it's a difficult and hard lesson to learn, becoming an artistic director changes your relationship with some colleagues and friends. You may or may not want to hire them, which can add tension, and you often cannot share information or discuss problems, because of confidentiality concerns. You can and should rely upon your managing director and your staff leaders. Also, realize that you now have a new group of colleagues with whom you can talk; these are your fellow artistic directors (especially those not in your community). Don't hesitate to ask them for advice, share problems, frustrations, and struggles. Contact those that you have worked for and/or admired. Call them regularly and talk with them at theatre conferences and performances.

As you work with staff and company, you will hear the delightfully strong opinions of theatre people! If you ask, they will tell you how things didn't work in the past and how things could work better in the future. These comments are often complaints or criticisms of your predecessor. Some are justified; some are not. To me, this situation can resemble a troubled divorce, when the aftershocks are still roiling those left behind. Listen for common themes and patterns behind the stories. Resist the temptation to allow these comments to continue; they may make you feel better about your expertise and experience, but they are not about you. Set a date for staff to "sunset" all negative or anguished stories about the past. Shift their focus to the future—namely, your artistic vision. How can they help achieve it? How can you support them? What can we create together?

Artistic directorships are all-consuming and endlessly stimulating; expect long hours, days, and weeks. At the same time, set boundaries on your time, effort, and energy. Although tempting, working longer and harder is not a long-term recipe for success; don't assume that you can achieve more by yourself. Above all, take care of yourself, your partner, and family. Find the time and space to recharge yourself.

Enjoy, learn, grow, keep the passion, and make a difference!

Conclusion

My inspiration for this book emerged from my own struggles figuring out how to get a job and then advance as a freelance director. My motivation only increased when I became an artistic director at three theatres, learned on the job, and hired many directors. I hope and trust you found my perspective and advice in this book useful as you pursue a professional career in stage directing.

The writing of the book has reminded me that parts of directing cannot be taught (especially in a book). One topic is the last step in creating a production that elevates a good show into an excellent one. I've tried metaphors and descriptions, such as "bringing the ship into port," and have listed questions to explore, but acknowledge that it is hard to explain or to teach this transformation from enjoyable to transcendent theatre. When I review the handful of shows that I have directed which have achieved that level of artistic success, I realize that I cannot always define what I did or what happened, except that I held an inner conviction that we as a collective could achieve something special. The success was always based upon the contributions of many, many people, and the breakthrough ideas came from lots of places—an usher's comment, a student audience's unusual response, an actor or crew member as well as the experienced and talented designers, gifted writers and composers, and more. Much to the delight and consternation of the cast, the crew, and the creative team, I kept trying ideas and giving more and more specific direction long into previews . . . until that moment when the entire company took over the show. And something magical happened.

Indeed, my best work often emerged as much from my intuition, instinct, and imagination as my intellectual understanding. As my mastery of directing theatre matured, I began to find the work endlessly relevant in my own life—finding meaning and connection in the process of directing. Each new show seemed to reveal another part of what it means to be human. Over time, I also discovered that I didn't really have a prescriptive set of actions that I or anyone can take that will ensure the show that I am directing gathers speed and takes off into flight. Instead, I have relied upon the dream and the hope that this production will, greatly enriched by the ideas, insights, and talents of my many, many collaborators over the years, succeed beyond the sum of its parts. Many people have helped me succeed as a director and artistic director—the playwrights, composers, lyricists, book writers, actors, designers, craftspeople, dramaturgs, crews, managers, trustees and donors. They bolstered my courage and illuminated my path. This reminds me that our job ultimately is to find a worthy theatrical story, preach a vision, and gather the people to bring it to life.

Our globalized, technological world now appears to be driven by capitalism and corporate profits, and the theatre often is dismissed as irrelevant or unnecessary. I disagree. As much as I enjoy the artistry and entertainment of films and television, cable and web programs, the live theatre remains a highly potent communal experience. As our digital devices and apps use ever more sophisticated ways to capture our attention every day, the theatrical performance battles against the inherent disconnect of the technological revolution. I have no illusions about the fragility of our art form or the considerable headwinds the theatre faces in today's world, but I also have spent my career watching the impact of live theatre performances on audiences. Although they gravitate most easily to musicals and light comedies, they talk about and remember best the shows that touch their hearts, open their eyes, stimulate their minds, and even stir their souls. Once they engage fully, we have an audience willing to respond, empathize, understand, and recognize. This transformative power of the theatre is what makes us feared and even hated, but it is also what makes us appreciated and loved. For many, we are an artistic window on a world which can be so difficult to comprehend.

Whatever level of directing in the theatre you attain, I hope you will treat it as a calling rather than a job—as an art form rather than a vocation. Although we may not change the world with our work, I'm confident we can change people's lives for the better.

Best wishes and Godspeed!

Notes

1 The Big Leap

1. Pentabus Rural Theatre Company, About page, http://www.pentabus. co.uk/about-us [accessed May 20, 2018].
2. Junebug Productions, About page, https://junebugproductions.org/about/ [accessed May 20, 2018].
3. Theatre Development Fund, Information on TKTS ticket booths, https:// www.tdf.org/nyc/7/TKTS-ticket-booths [accessed May 20, 2018].
4. Online Theatre London, Society of London Theatre, information on TKTS, http://www.tkts.co.uk [accessed May 20, 2018].
5. D. Gewirtzman, "Schedule of Upcoming Live Theatre Broadcasts in Movie Theatres and on Television," *Playbill*, 2018, http://www.playbill.com/ article/schedule-of-upcoming-live-theatre-broadcasts-in-movie-theatres-and-on-television-com-322823 [accessed May 21, 2018].
6. New York Public Library for the Performing Arts, Locations page, https:// www.nypl.org/locations/lpa [accessed May 21, 2018].
7. Victoria & Albert Museums, Theatre & Performance Collections page, https://www.vam.ac.uk/collections/theatre-performance [accessed May 21, 2018].
8. Shakespeare's Globe Theatre, Exhibition page: http://www. shakespearesglobe.com/exhibition-and-tour [accessed May 21, 2018].
9. The Theatre Museum, Facebook page, https://www.facebook.com/ thetheatremuseum [accessed May 21, 2018].
10. Regional Theatre Young Directors Scheme, http://www.rtyds.co.uk/ [accessed June 28, 2018].
11. The Icarus Theatre Collective, About page, http://www.icarustheatre.co.uk/ about_icarus.html [accessed May 30, 2018].
12. New Dramatists, Welcome page, http://newdramatists.org/ [accessed June 28, 2018].
13. Lark Theatre Company, Home page, http://newdramatists.org/ [accessed May 30, 2018].
14. Playwright Center, About page, https://pwcenter.org/about [accessed May 31, 2018].

15. The Eugene O'Neill Theater Center, About page, http://www.theoneill.org/about-us/ [accessed May 31, 2018].
16. Birmingham Repertory Theatre, Archived online, http://self.gutenberg.org/articles/eng/Birmingham_Repertory_Theatre [accessed June 10, 2018].

2 Understanding the Business of Theatre

1. Equity, Landing page, https://www.equity.org.uk [accessed May 31, 2018].
2. Equity, Director's section, https://www.equity.org.uk/directors/ [accessed May 31, 2018].
3. Society of London Theatres, Homepage, http://solt.co.uk/ [accessed May 31, 2018].
4. Theatre UK, Homepage, https://uktheatre.org/ [accessed May 31, 2018].
5. Society of Directors and Choreographers, Homepage, http://www.sdcweb.org/ [accessed May 31, 2018].
6. Laura Penn, letter to the editor, *American Theatre*, May 3, 2017, https://www.americantheatre.org/2017/05/03/letter-to-the-editor-compensation-isnt-a-competition/ [accessed June 10, 2018].
7. Stage Directors UK, "The SDUK Report on Theatre Directors' Pay," January 2015, http://www.stagedirectorsuk.com/fee-report/ [accessed May 31, 2018].

5 Rehearsals in the Studio

1. Anne Bogart, *A Director Prepares: Seven Essays on Art and Theatre* (New York & London, Routledge, 2001), 124.

9 Directing New Plays and Musicals

1. *All the Way* (Tony Award for Best Play), *The Kentucky Cycle* (Pulitzer Prize), *Building the Wall*, and films *All the Way* and *Hacksaw Ridge* (with Andrew Knight).
2. Playwright of *The Great Leap*, *The King of the Yees*, *Cambodian Rock Band*, *in a Word*, and *The Hatmaker's Wife*, among others, produced at the

Goodman Theatre, South Coast Rep., Atlantic Theatre Company, Seattle Rep., Denver Center, Center Theatre Group, etc.

3.   *One Night in Miami, Little Black Shadows,* and more, at the Donmar Warehouse, Baltimore Center Stage, South Coast Rep., Denver Center Theatre Company.

10 Nurturing Your Art and Yourself

1.   Jim Jarmusch, "Things I've Learned," *MovieMaker Magazine,* Winter, June 5, 2013, https://www.moviemaker.com/archives/series/things_learned/ jim-jarmusch-5-golden-rules-of-moviemaking/ [accessed May 31, 2018].

2.   Skylar Mason, "Center Stage: William Partlan on the Joy of Bringing a Play to Life," *The State Press,* April 16, 2016, http://www.statepress.com/ article/2016/04/asu-center-stage-william-partlan [accessed May 21, 2018].

11 Leading a Theatre . . . or Not

1.   Noel Tichy and Ram Charan, "Speed, Simplicity, Self-Confidence: An Interview with Jack Welch," *Harvard Business Review,* September–October, 1989, https://hbr.org/1989/09/speed-simplicity-self-confidence-an-interview-with-jack-welch [accessed June 10, 2018].

2.   Alliance Theatre, Mission/Vision page, https://alliancetheatre.org/content/ missionvision [accessed June 10, 2018].

3.   Oregon Shakespeare Festival, Mission & Values page, https://www. osfashland.org/company/mission-and-values.aspx [accessed June 10, 2018].

4.   Royal Court Theatre, About Us page, https://royalcourttheatre.com/about/ [accessed May 31, 2018].

5.   Michael Kaiser, "Artistic Directors Versus Executive Directors," *Huffington Post,* September 24, 2009, http://www.huffingtonpost.com/michael-kaiser/ artistic-directors-versus_b_264140.html [accessed May 31, 2018].

Further Reading

Arthur Bartow, *The Director's Voice: Twenty-One Interviews* (New York: Theatre Communications Group, 1993).

Anne Bogart, *What's the Story: Essays about Art, Theater and Storytelling* (Oxford & New York: Routledge, 2014).

Anne Bogart, *Conversations with Anne: Twenty-Two Interviews* (New York: Theatre Communications Group, 2012).

Michael Bloom, *Thinking Like a Director* (New York: Faber and Faber, 2001).

Peter Brook, *Tip of the Tongue* (London: Nick Hern Books, 2017).

John Caird, *Theatre Craft: A Director's Practical Companion A to Z* (London: Faber and Faber, 1990).

Harold Clurman, *On Directing,* reissue (New York: Touchstone, 1997).

Alexander Dean and Laurence Carra, *Fundamentals of Directing*, 5th ed. (Long Grove, IL: Waveland Press, 2009).

Nicholas Hytner, *Balancing Acts: Behind the Scenes at London's National Theatre* (London: Knopf, 2017).

Christopher Innes and Maria Shevtsova, *The Cambridge Introduction to Theatre Directing* [Cambridge Introductions to Literature] (Cambridge: Cambridge University Press, 2013).

Robert Knopf, *Script Analysis for Theatre: Tools for Interpretation, Collaboration and Production* (London & New York: Bloomsbury Methuen Drama, 2017).

Jason Loewith, *The Director's Voice: Twenty Interviews, Vol. 2* (New York: Theatre Communications Group, 1993).

Todd London, *An Ideal Theater: Founding Vision for a New American Art* (New York: Theatre Communications Group, 2013).

Todd London, *The Artistic Home: Discussions with Artistic Directors of America's Institutional Theatres* (New York: Theater Communications Group, 1993).

Charles Ney, *Directing Shakespeare in America: Current Practices* (London & New York: Bloomsbury Arden Shakespeare, 2016).

Nancy Roche and Jaan Whitehead, *The Art of Governance*, "Foreword" by Joanne Woodward (New York: Theatre Communications Group, 2005).

Abigail Rokison-Woodall, *Shakespeare in the Theatre: Nicholas Hytner* (London & New York: Bloomsbury Arden Shakespeare, 2017).

Jim Volz, *Working in American Theatre*, 2nd revised ed. (New York & London, Bloomsbury Methuen Drama, 2011).

Jim Volz, *Introduction to Arts Management* (New York & London: Bloomsbury Methuen Drama, 2017).

About the Author

Kent Thompson is a theatre director, producer, educator and writer. He has led two major regional theatres in the US, the Denver Center Theatre Company from 2005 to 2017 and the Alabama Shakespeare Festival from 1989 to 2005. Thompson is an accomplished director of Shakespeare and classics as well as new plays. Widely known as an advocate, supporter, developer and producer of new plays and musicals, Thompson created two new play festivals: the Colorado New Play Summit and the Southern Writers' Project. In Denver, he also founded Off Center to explore immersive, innovative programming for millennials and The Women's Voices Fund to commission new plays by women. Thompson has commissioned more than 65 new plays and produced 48 world premieres. He served as Board president of Theatre Communications Group (the national organization for the American theatre), and has served on numerous peer panels, including Doris Duke Foundation, Andrew W. Mellon Foundation, Pew Charitable Trust, National Endowment for the Arts Theatre Panel (also Chair), and Fulbright Scholars Panel. He is currently a member of the Playwright Award Advisory Committee of the Harold and Mimi Steinberg Charitable Trust. He is a graduate of the College of William & Mary and the Guildhall School of Music & Drama in London.

Index